BATTLE CRY

*My Journey to Purpose
during My Biggest Storms*

J E N N I   L Y N N

Fulton Books
Meadville, PA

Published by Fulton Books 2024

ISBN 979-8-89427-349-5 (paperback)
ISBN 979-8-89427-350-1 (digital)

Printed in the United States of America

To my beautiful son, Jaxx
You are the light at the end of every storm,
and I will always reach for you!

Endorsements

A powerful, compelling memoir of a woman's battle to embrace self-love while conquering anxiety, depression, motherhood, and negative self-talk. Set on the journey to becoming closer to God, healing, past trauma, and accepting the love she never thought she deserved but always needed. Real and raw- she will forever be "Fierce One."

—Missy Rodgers

Inspiring and dynamic. An honest and heartfelt memoir of the realities of life and the strength and will to overcome obstacles and trials with faith and grace of God.

—Joyce Tringhese

The tiny author with the biggest voice! This book will help you get through your hardest storms and help you climb your biggest mountains. Jenni has been in my life for over thirty years, and she will not only wow you with her story, but you will see her true heart shine throughout this book. May it help you face your demons and slay your dragons all while getting to know a little more about my dearest friend.

—Alix Hertel

In *Battle Cry: My Journey to Purpose During My Biggest Storms*, Jenni shares her life struggles with raw honesty. Her openness regarding her faith and how it brings her through her struggles is inspiring. Her story is a compelling narrative of resilience, triumph, and the human spirit. Jenni Lynn takes readers on a journey through her most challenging moments and greatest achievements, offering insights and suggestions to her readers for any challenges they may face. A must-read for anyone seeking motivation and a deeper understanding of the extraordinary paths some lives take.
—Tricia Myers, HR director and friend, Hynes Industries Inc.

Truly inspiring. In a powerful and deeply personal journal, Jenni opens her life so that you can save yours. Jenni's story of self-discovery, finding light in the darkness each of us faces in life, never asking "why" but instead trusting in God's plan. Relying on her faith in God, fearlessness, inner strength, and reflection, Jenni demonstrates how light shines through the cracks in our lives. A moving but practical guide to finding happiness and peace from within.
—Rick Organ, CEO and president, Hynes Industries Inc.

This book is a great lesson in perseverance and never giving up, I love this because Jenni bares her soul, and really shares with the reader what life was like. However, she never gave up and it makes me feel like I too can climb every mountain.
—Arlette Slater

Contents

Introduction

I am not a victim of my life. What I went through pulled a warrior out of me and it is my greatest honor to be her!

—Rupi Kaur

Thirty-four years! It took me thirty-four years and many battles to climb the courage train to write this novel. When God says, "Do it!" you do it, so here I am. Not only is my story empowering, but the struggles I faced and the battles God got me through gave me a lot of breakthroughs I didn't think I could conquer. Some of them I honestly didn't see me getting through because fear and anxiety took over! But God had a different plan for me—and a good one at that. I wouldn't trade what I've been through for the world. What I got out of all of it was not only my beautiful son, Jaxx, but *strength, courage, fearlessness, power, purpose, self-worth, hope, a better future, and most importantly a stronger relationship with God!*

Doors opened for me in all kinds of ways starting in 2021 to the man of my dreams, taking that leap of faith in a new job, building a better and healthier life for Jaxx, finally being able to talk to a therapist and open up to someone.

But with all that good news always comes moments of struggle. We have all been there, done that, and I have moments that make me question what I am doing with my life, even when things are perfect. Sometimes a curveball comes swinging in, and we must learn how to swerve. I've become pretty good at swerving and handling my emotions, but I'm not perfect, so I'd have to say I still have to work on myself, and that's okay—that's life and nobody ever said it was going to be easy, just worth it! And everything I have right now is well worth it all!

I asked myself many times while trying to think about why I wanted to write this book and what was going to motivate me to tell a lot of people my story and some pretty dark parts of my personal life, and frankly it was very easy to process—*closure for myself and helping everyone else not only find their light but their purpose and their climb to victory during their most difficult storms*!

I have struggled with crippling anxiety, depression, negativity on myself for decades, and I knew doing this was inspiring for myself to break free from all of it with the help of the Word of God, being fearless and helping others to be inspired by my stories, and reaching out to the families who need it most that struggle with the same battles I have faced. And let's be honest here, I will probably face for the rest of my life with *control* and *surrender* by my side, which I will get into more in the chapters ahead.

Family is everything to me, but sometimes family is what breaks your heart the most and what also gives you the most strength and willpower to get up and keep going!

If there is anything I have learned in the past thirty-four years of my life thus far, it's not the getting up that hurts when you have been bruised to no end internally; it's the scars that are left behind that remind you of what happened in that moment. Yep, we all have them! Because guess what? Nobody is perfect but the big man above, and I give him all the glory and praise for reaching down in the waters and saving me from drowning *many* times when I didn't think I could surface. Most of all, I wouldn't have my son if it weren't for him. Jaxx is my saving grace, and I count my blessings every day for being able to be his mom.

God will pull you from the depths of the ocean, he will! He did it for me, and he can do it for you. There is nothing in this world that you can't conquer or prosper from. If you can find the strength every morning to get up and keep going, then you can do anything life swings your way; even if that ball comes flying, just keep swerving!

Here is one of my favorite verses during my divorce, and still is one. I use it daily during any storm that comes my way or anytime I feel helpless. "*He trains my hands for battle; My arms can bend a bow of bronze*" (Psalm 18:34). I think this verse is so incredibly powerful, which makes me feel strong in my heart. All I can picture is my whole body bending a bow of bronze on top of my mountain, screaming my *battle cry* with the strength God has given me during my storms to help me get through the toughest and most challenging battles of my life. I still think about this verse on days I feel weak and need some strength to remind me, "You got this, Jen, bend the bow."

Even as a little girl, he trained me to be stronger and prepared me for what he knew was coming into my life! Isn't that amazing? That we can look at what we went through or currently going through and think, *Okay? Why did that happen to me? Did I deserve to feel all that pain? Why was I sexually molested as a little girl, rejected, abandoned, looked down on? Why was I cheated on repeatedly with multiple partners by my ex? Why did I have unfair judgement, fear, doubt, jealousy, insecure anger, and bitterness?* Yes, it was supposed to happen to help me get through the next one, and then the next one, and guess what? The next one! I don't know about you, but for me, they increasingly got worse. But each one made me stronger, and I have no regrets on any of them.

I hope during each chapter, each sentence, each word, I can get you to live fearless, live stronger, courageous, power through your storm, and hopefully in not only the Word of God but the strength to open your eyes every morning to a new day and think to yourself, *It's going to be okay. I can do this…I can withstand any obstacle life throws at me!* You are all beautiful in my eyes, even during the pain and ugly moments that make us vulnerable. I hope you choose to *live!*

At the end of each chapter, I want you to say one positive thing about yourself! I know for myself it was hard to be positive about who I was and who I was becoming during the hardest parts of my life. I hated looking at myself in the mirror.

It made my mom sad one day when I told her I hate looking at myself when I just saw disgust every day, asking myself what I am doing wrong, and as a mother myself, I knew I wouldn't want to hear my son say those things about himself, and I needed to change my outlook on how I talked to myself.

I started writing positive things on sticky notes and putting them all over my bathroom, bedroom, kitchen, and hallways so I could read them in every room I entered to remind myself, *"I am worthy!"* And so are you! So get a sticky pad with bright colors and a pen, and after each chapter, write a positive thing about yourself or an improvement you want to accomplish and stick it wherever your heart desires, so at the end of each chapter, you can reference back to it when you are in a time of need.

Let me empower you with my battles and my story to let you know it's okay to get out of that dark shadow, it's okay to keep climbing your mountain. Because I'll be waiting for you at the top with my hands stretched out, ready to celebrate your victory! You are worth every struggle God puts in your life to help you get to your *light*!

Welcome to my journey. I can't wait to inspire you and bring peace to your heart! Get up and stand tall and let me hear your *battle cry!*

Millennial

*I didn't have a good beginning in life, but I
fully intend to have a great finish.*

—Joyce Meyer

Jennifer Lynn Hull, born December 3, 1989, in Youngstown, Ohio,
at St. Elizabeth Hospital. A millennial was born. That's right, a
millennial. The kind that soaked in all the amazing '90s memories of watching the *Rugrats*, playing *Sonic the Hedgehog* on Sega,
Nickelodeon, Disney movies… I wanted to be Pocahontas in "Colors
of the Wind." I had a pink Razr flip phone, the glitter jeans that flared
out, Backstreet Boys, N'SYNC, Britney Spears, Spice Girls, renting
new movies from Blockbuster because Netflix and chill wasn't a thing
yet. I was your typically girly-girly, and I could go on and on and
on, so I'll stop there so my fellow millennials can bask in on those
beautiful memories!

Thirty-four years young and four feet ten to be exact. I love
reading, playing music on a daily especially when I'm cleaning, col-
lecting all the old versions of the *Nancy Drew* books that I read and
grew up on… Anything vintage has my heart. Singing is a soul pro-
tector, dancing is freeing. My favorite color is orange. I love Diet
Pepsi. I highlight everything imaginable that needs my attention.
I enjoy planners, calendars, and notebooks; traveling on Corey's
Harley. Dragonflies are my spirit animal. My son is my twin. I have
seven different laughs for different reasons and only one person
knows them. I want to travel the world. I prefer mountains over the
ocean anytime of the day. Cotton balls freak me out. I cannot stand
the feeling or sight of velvet and corduroy. I am working a full-time

1

day job as a Human Resource Generalist at Hynes Industries, walking the trails and watching the same series over and over again.

Now let's take it back to 1989, in the hospital that started it all and what really started my journey in life—the first battle cry out of the womb.

The Lord has done it this very day; Let us rejoice today and be glad. (Psalm 118–24 NIV)

As my mom was going into labor, my dad insisted I stay until the Raiders game was over against their all-time rivals, the Denver Broncos. Sure enough, we won a victory game, and here I came with a victory cry into the world. As a baby and growing up, I watched and wore all Raiders gear, and to this day, I am a die-hard Raiders fan. Everyone would and still does ask me why the Raiders; if you weren't born there, well, that is why! I was an only sibling until my brother was born June 12, 1994, residing in Columbiana, Ohio, that is now known as "the nicest place to live in America." I beg to differ; there weren't any mountains. We lived in a beautiful home on Blueberry Drive, and my brother and I both went to Columbiana schools until we graduated in 2008 and 2012.

Family

Family means the world to me, and I will say that I am closer to my family than I ever was before. No family is perfect, and there is always going to be drama in every household. Mine came with some baggage, but God knew we were strong enough to take what he was giving us and run with it. I can't say they haven't broken my heart more than once, and I have hurt them as well with words and actions because I am also not perfect, but it's what molded me into the person I am today and what has made me strong, so I wouldn't change any of it to get what I have now in my life. Even when things got sticky, I found my faith to get past my waves during the moments when family wasn't quite there for all of it or could see what was happening in my wake. I still love them even during the dark parts!

Give thanks to the Lord, for he is good; his love endures forever. (Psalm 106:1 NIV)

Revelation: *God will pull you from the depths of the ocean, he will! He did it for me, he can do it for you! Declare it, pray on it, post it on your sticky note, say it out loud in front of the mirror! I'm rooting for you!*

Breathe

You have to learn to drop it.

—Steven Furtick

It has been a passion of mine to help others understand that the struggle does not define your life but that it is something we should work on overcoming to help us move past what we fear the most.

With that being said, I plan to just put it all out there. I have to be vulnerable here in these chapters, but I think the vulnerability is what some people need to read and need to hear—a storyline of what could save someone's life who has a hard time getting past what they can't see right in front them, helping them to open that door to clarity and freedom. We all want that. We all crave it. We just have to get there. I want to help you with the faith I keep so dear to my heart and talk about how normal it is to feel like faith isn't on your side. You can feel both and still be okay knowing that we just need that push. I promise that the mountaintop isn't as high as you think; it's all about the perspective that lies ahead of you, so keep climbing! I know I am still climbing mine.

Let's get down to basics here, shall we, because let's be honest, I am a mess—always have been, always will be. I have come to terms with the fact that life does go on, even on the bad days, because it is not a bad life, just a bad day.

I don't know about you, but I talk to myself *a lot!* Not just here and there but first thing in the morning and right before I close my eyes to go to sleep at night. I even talk to myself while taking a shower. It's like a pep talk when I'm cleansing the negativity from myself. I thank those thoughts talking to me because sometimes they calm me down. It's just me saying, "You got this, Jenni, nothing to fear."

Talking back and forth, though, can kind of put you in a sticky situation, depending on what is bothering me at the moment. Like, for example, my relationship is amazing, and I have the most incredible man in my life who loves me and my son, but with going through a traumatic divorce and past comes some weird mental breakdowns and always thinking the worst when in reality there is nothing wrong. So I put negative thoughts in my head to make me overthink what I have no business of even thinking because it's God's plan, not mine in the end. I literally tell myself to stop, or I am going to be in deep waters. I know that sounds kind of crazy, but it's the only way I can get out of a thought I don't want to be in.

I can go into a dark place that I know nobody wants to enter; it is the place that takes me down memory lane and not the happy kind, but the kind that makes-your-skin-crawl-and-never-take-me-back-there-again kind of memories! So let me tell you this! It doesn't matter how many people I vent to, talk to, cry, scream at to get my point across; the dark side always comes out to play. And when this happens, I have to go to my happy place that I will say is easy for me to do for the moment, just to get back on track. Without that happy thought, my mind will slip into the abyss. Panic mode is not fun, so with my happy place comes the calm somber moments of breathing. Breathe until that smile comes back to your face. I promise you it will come back once you learn to breathe through every negative moment. Even a good laugh comes a long way; laughing is the best medicine for anyone. Some of the funniest comedians like Robin Williams created a life of laughter to mask the depression he was sustaining in his life, and none of us even knew he was struggling; we just watched him inspire us all by how he made us laugh. And now he is forever a legend and forever remembered. It made me sad to find out he was internally and mentally in a bad space for so long, someone who seemed like he had it all together. When in reality we never really have it all figured out, or together, we coast and find the faith to reach for God when he is louder.

I wish for Robin that he heard him louder than ever before so he could still be with us today to make us laugh. Now we only have his memories. How impactful is that to not physically know someone but feel so deeply for them at the end of their life, that their calling was bigger, and he made it known that laughter was the only way to keep surviving.

I think to myself constantly that there are a lot of people in this world who have it worse than others, including myself. I become all dramatic and have to tell myself that my life could be way worse, and I am extremely blessed even when I feel like a mess. When you feel yourself drifting, just think, *Could this be worse? Am I being too uptight over something I can't even control right now?* It's a hard situation to get out of, I know! But we must find ways to dig ourselves out of the ground and plant our feet back on the surface.

I fear a lot of things, and my anxiety is beyond intense that can spiral into a panic attack! I try to live fearlessly, and some days I can accomplish that task. But other days I can't even think straight, and all I want to do is lie in bed and not get out until the crippling anxiety and depression seeps away from me. I can be extremely positive to anyone who needs my help, but when it comes time for that dark side to start knocking on my door, I don't take my own advice very seriously because I know all too well that trauma can and will eat you alive! That's why I write and read a lot; I have to go into a new place in my head to get out of my own to then go back to that door I was in before the black cloud came and reached and grabbed at my tree branches.

At the end of the day though, I don't let that feeling stay with me. God always finds a way to clear that path, so I don't stay stuck in that rut forever.

Another thing I like to do that I put in my head that work wonders is going to the sink and splashing ice-cold water on my face. This is usually what I do first thing in the morning when I wake up, like a culture shock to my nerves! It's seriously rewarding after a few splashes just to get myself back to maybe a little bit of sanity, so I can get back to work and feel normal. Yeah! Yeah! I know what's normal in this day and age we live in is nothing is normal, not even going out to the grocery store to get milk and bread! I mean, come on, we can't even sneeze anymore in public without someone mean-mugging you in the line next to you!

Covid destroyed a lot of things and put way too much fear and separation on all of us, so no nothing is normal, and I just hope we can get back to a better place together. And with maybe a little hope from my words of wisdom, I can help spread that to all of you. Let's start talking not only nicer to each other but to ourselves.

Get out of your own way so God has the lane to continue!

We just say stuff—we say things without taking a breather. We must learn to breathe and think before you take that next one.

I am very guilty for saying things to my loved ones without thinking, and it's honestly a trigger response for me, and I am working on this every day.

After the damage is done, I think, *I forgot to breathe. Lord, help me fix this. I surrender this all to you. It is out of my hands now. I promise I will try to breathe next time. My tongue got the best of me and got in my way.*

We also think, *Why are they not saying anything? Why are they silent? Let them breathe first and then maybe they won't come at you with an attack, and then you can appreciate the silence. The conversation will be better because you let them think. Don't be offended by their silent mouth and mind—God is talking them through the situation, and he is continuing to work on them, and he is at the same time working on you in preparation for that un-silent conversation that is about to happen.*

Being offended is a decision. Breathe before you say something you will regret and surrender what is to happen to God. Let him finish the work. I promise you will breathe better.

With faith you can do anything, and I hope these chapters can be light out of your darkest storms. Remember, storms come and go—they come so the rain can wash away the pain you are currently in and only clear skies ahead for a new chapter to begin. How refreshing does that sound? I sure do like the sound of that for myself.

A summary of the trauma I have been through and have worked past are the following:

- *Parents' divorce*
- *Family drinking trauma*
- *Secrets and deception*
- *Sexually molested by family*
- *High school bullying*
- *Being disowned*
- *Cheated on*
- *Rejected by family and friends*
- *Divorce*
- *Self-loathing*
- *Manipulation*
- *Narcissism and lies*

There you go… It's a twisted maze, the kind that every corner turned felt like the same one I was stepping into until that new door was presented. That's when I knew God said, "It's time to move on to the next chapter, walk through, and see what I have in store for you," that I walked through fearlessly, and I tried not to ask too many questions because it was going to happen regardless.

All thanks to my amazing Corey and my son, Jaxx. My son saved me time and time again, and Corey found me in just the right moment in my life when I needed him the most. He came in with a flashlight and found me in the dark corner of that maze I was in. But sometimes darkness tries to still grab ahold of me, and I just swat!

That's the scary thing about the mind, it's hard to move past and shut off what thoughts can say to you. You probably know this all too well because we all encounter these things one time or another, which can send you into an overthinking overload. Train your heart to help you talk out of that overthinking mindset and into something positive. It's hard sometimes, I know, but God will strengthen your mind to get to that point because he doesn't want you in that space to begin with.

Breathe yourself out of that maze. Don't be afraid of what's around the corner; it could surprise you but learn to embrace it with open arms to the potential you know you have.

Revelation: *Do you have a maze you are struggling with? Write on a sticky how you got through your maze and what came into your life to get you out of it and what you did after. Keep turning those corners, you never know what's on the other side.*

Girl, Get Up

Life is tough but so are you.

Sometimes I have moments of pure dread, like my body just wants to shut down, my head is pounding, and all I can think about is what next emotion is going to hit me in the face when I least expect it. That's called anxiety!

This may sound crazy but what helps my anxiety is a cold bottle of Diet Pepsi. Something about the fizz in my mouth eases the thoughts in my head and wakes me up.

I sometimes have literal thoughts that I am a horrible mother to Jaxx *when I know I am not* that person at all, not even close. I think to myself that even the slightest negative outcome is me being a lousy mother and that I am not teaching Jaxx anything. I think that is a horrible thought to have because they say, when you doubt, it means in reality you are doing everything right. If you feel this way also, you aren't alone, and you are a good parent to your child. They look up to you in ways we may never understand because their love is so unconditional, and we should learn that from them. We teach them, and in return they can teach us!

I used to get in this state of mind that what my ex-husband did to me is because I am nothing but worthless. Then I ask myself why anyone would want to do hurtful things like he did to me or anyone for that matter. Then I think about the beautiful son I get to hold and look at, and I can breathe better knowing my purpose in this life is because of that little boy. I wouldn't have him if I didn't go through the things that I did, or if I didn't take the path I was in to get to be his mom. That is what I call a bittersweet symphony.

I also think about the man in my life who loves me unconditionally, even when he met me at the lowest point in my life. He still
stood by my side even when I thought every day I was failing; he saw
nothing but brightness in my eyes when I could only see darkness.
He brought me back to life and reminded me that I am not only a
good person but worthy of so much more than I thought possible.
Something like what I have is hard to come across and timing is
everything.

The problem with feeling these things is how can something be
so wonderful and feel so right and then thinking, *God gave me this
perfect life with answered prayers, he can take it all away*—that scares
me half to death. I don't want to sit in my room wondering, *What
if this all goes away? What will I do? Will I hit an even harder wall
than I ever have?* Because if that's the case, then I feel paralyzed at
the thought of how I will get up again. That is way too dark for me
to even fathom, so I rely on God's presence to get me through those
thoughts because, with him, anything is possible—the maker of all
things good in my life and in yours. When you feel like you are falling off the edge of a cliff, you need to give yourself that talk and that
reassurance that it is okay to step back and think about what could
be worse and how you can make it better. Give yourself that grace
you so badly need.

I know there are times when I want to be left alone by everyone
in my life, completely want total silence to think and reflect on what
I need to do in the moment, to make my mind work again, to repro-
gram what is better mentally, to breathe a little easier and make my
steps go forward. And that, my friends, is a hard task when you are
battling with your own mind, constantly thinking of the worst-case
scenario.

I read two different kinds of genres of books. One is the mys-
terious and thriller knock-you-off-your-feet kind of novels, and then
there is the spiritual, motivated, mentor kind of novels. Complete
opposites of each other, right? The reason for that is the thriller ones
take me to a place I probably wouldn't want to be a part of in real
life and makes me appreciate what I have, especially when they are
nonfiction ones—I go into a different world that isn't mine. The

motivational ones help keep me balanced and put me in check on how to get out of the funk I may be in. Pastor Steven Furtick and Holly Furtick take me out of that one real quick with his novels and podcasts. He's serious and funny at the same time; who wouldn't want to listen and read something that makes you belly laugh and cry all in one hour of your day? I also love how raw he is. He is completely transparent to the battles he still currently goes through. Here is a man that thousands and thousands of people look up to, and he isn't afraid to say, "I am not perfect, and I will always be a work in progress, using God's leading words to help others." To me, that is so powerful, and someone I constantly want and continue to follow and listen in on.

Do you have something in your life that is your only constant to pull you away from something that feels like you are suffocating? Even if it's jumping on that treadmill, writing in a journal, eating that yogurt first thing in the morning, watching that movie that gives you hope, ordering that takeout you love so much, planning that vacation you have been dreaming of, riding that bike on the trail, or walking that trail—as long as you can find that motivation, then you have it handled for the most part. All in all, sometimes getting up is the hardest part of our day, but we need to focus on the things that help us rise and see a new morning. Trust me, there are days I don't get up, and it takes me hours to find that willpower, but eventually something gravitates a pull to give me that nudge to start. It's not a bad life, just a bad day, and we still have tomorrow!

Let me tell you a story about when it was hard for me to get out of bed, and I remember this like it was yesterday. I didn't leave my bed except to go to the bathroom for two days. I know, gross, but it was a rough two days for me mentally.

I was in the process of moving into my new apartment at the end of the year in 2020, after moving out of my house and starting anew while in the works of my divorce. I was anxious and honestly excited to start anew with Jaxx and build something special with him; starting fresh is the mindset I was after. I was all moved, and my birthday in December was approaching. I get sad when that day comes up because, for some odd reason, nothing ever goes well for me. It was falling on a Sunday, and that weekend, I stayed home and really didn't do anything but hang around. But after the fact when it came time for the days I knew I wasn't going to have Jaxx or see him, I took sick days from work and stayed home. I woke up, and I tell you, I cried like I've never cried before. Yes, I did just that—swollen eyes and all! I watched TV in my room, slept, got up to go to the bathroom, went back and cried. I wanted so badly to hold my baby after being able to do it every day to not; that kind of change in my life was hard to handle. I was feeling unworthy and questioned every-thing about everything I did and said. I asked God to hold me in those moments. I was scared and prayed for him to bring me some-one that wouldn't hurt me, someone I could trust, while thinking, *Is it even possible anymore for someone to love so deeply and care so much that the thought of hurting them isn't even imaginable?* I didn't think it was fathomable or real.

Mind going, not eating, head pounding, eyes hurting—I was a hot mess, a literal hot mess!

After day two, I took another sick day and lay in bed until I had to get Jaxx because it was my day to have him. Just in that moment, I said that I needed to get up to shower, get cleaned up, eat something, and get my energy back. I couldn't get Jaxx looking like this or feeling this way. I cannot show any weakness around him, so I said what I still say to this day and my biggest battle cry, *"GIRL, GET UP!"*

Pretty sure, I said it over, and over, and over again out loud until I pushed my body out of the covers and got it together. After that, I still wasn't okay, but I found the strength to do it. My little boy, he needed me and, to this day, still needs me and always will, so I will continue to get up for him and provide, even when the going gets tough.

I am telling you this because some people may think weakness is pathetic and you are nothing if you are weak, especially in the mind. We need to go through those trials, so we can learn and know what to do in order to survive those weaknesses, build the strength we know is inside all of us. We need to understand that even when we feel weak, God has the strength of an army to hold us up and have faith in him.

On the days I still feel like I am about to have that same moment, I write on a sticky note or multiple ones—I keep a spare at my office desk—*"Girl, get up!"* and keep it close by as a reminder that I am not that girl in the bed, lying there for two days, wondering if I will ever feel better. I am not her. I am not defined by her or anything in my past! I am a better version of what is to come and what has already approached my life, and the same goes for you! *Get up, get going, don't look back, and don't stop!*

Revelation: *Sticky note time! Get it out and write the last memory you have—even if it was five minutes ago—of the last negative thought you had, and what did you do to release that pressure? Was it a song that makes everything go away? A funny series you watch when you need a laugh? A mentor in a podcast? A book you haven't opened in a while because you got sidetracked with being busy? Go to that happy place and don't let go of it!*

Get Out of Your Head

I love when God interrupts my thoughts and
reminds me that battle is not mine but his.

Have you ever been in your head so intently you feel like a crazy person? Like every situation in your mind makes you feel like you are doing everything wrong and every move you make. Or the little devil and angel on your shoulders we know all too well keep bickering on what we should or shouldn't do.

This is the biggest battle of my life, being in my head about every little thing, and I mean everything! From what happens at work to being a mom, relationships with family and friends, I am always thinking the worst, and it can be exhausting. I know I am not alone on this, and I really do dislike thinking worst-case scenarios or overthinking something that is out of my control. God is in control, not me, and I've learned to let go of what is not in my grasp and hand it over to him.

I argue with my mind. I tell myself, "Jenni, you are completely fine, breathe and calm down!" Easier said than done, right? I know. It sucks being stuck in that mud.

I learned to control it a lot better than I used to, and I mean I have found ways to let it go, talk it out of my head, read a good book, open up my Bible, write in my journal, vent it out to someone or anyone I know that will make it better, even if I feel like they think, *Geez, she talks way to much!* I know I do. I validate that I ramble on, but then I thought that trauma has caused me to think this way.

There are moments I don't think the thoughts in my head will go away, and when I'm alone, I'll cry for hours or get the worst chest pains of my life. It's usually unbearable and, quite frankly, very embarrassing if anyone is around. And then this is when I don't want to talk to anyone and end up isolating myself. When this happens, it's a bad position for me, and I work really hard to get out of that funk before soon enough someone is going to realize something is wrong beyond the point of a panic attack. I know typing that sounds nuts, and yes, I am currently in therapy to work past this because sometimes things we are going through need more help past the yoga we do in the morning or rituals. We just need that extra step and help to talk to someone who is nonjudgmental to the lifestyle you are in.

When we are in our own minds, we tend to daydream, right? It's something we all do—get into a place we feel safe then daydream about what we want and where we want to be.

I do a lot of this and have more than one. I daydream on maybe getting engaged *again* and having that real wedding I deserve. And I don't mean the real wedding with all the things around me because, yes, I have been married, and I did all the things, but that is not what is important after marrying someone you thought cared for you. You look at marriage in a different way. Whether that be I never want to be married again or I want to be married because I don't know how it truly feels like to have the real deal until it's right in front of me. My marriage was fake, and I was robbed. I can say I have the real deal now. *Finally!* And so I daydream about having it all with him. It's a daydream that I don't like getting out of because it makes me smile… Just thinking about my dad and Jaxx walking me down the aisle and finally saying, "This is what it is supposed to feel like," while my dad smiles with tears in his eyes and Jaxx gets excited to just be holding my hand while our families smile and think, *She did it!* My mom would be so proud, everyone would be. But the reality is I would be proud of myself that I was able to have faith in the process of letting someone in to love me, all of me; even the negative parts give me a chance to have that fairy-tale ending. Knowing he feels the same way and we can't live our lives without each other, that's the ultimate end game right there and should be in a Disney movie. Okay, that made me laugh! That is the fairy tale that keeps on replaying in my mind.

But of course, the downside to that fairy tale is will it and can it come true? That's when I am in my head, and the happy parts turn into doubts of *Well, what if it doesn't happen to me? Will I get the chance to have it all?* I was cheated out of something I thought was right. I got the short end of the stick, and that didn't seem fair.

When that state of mind plays out, I get emotional and start thinking, *Am I worthy enough for someone to love me that much? I wasn't then, can I be now?* And well, I left my last marriage. It was my choice not to stay in a toxic environment, not only for myself but for Jaxx. When someone hurts you so badly, there is no going back, and I didn't, so now I live with this "in-your-head" scenario over and over again because of it.

If you are going through the same valley as me, I understand what and how you are feeling. Some of you may think, *Well, no, I don't ever want to be married again. It damaged me that much.* That is okay, and while you process how to get through that, in due time, whether you move on or you don't, I hope you still find your happy ending, even if that means traveling the world and doing it alone to come back to tell your story and get your closure! It is all about how you control that mind of yours. It can be a deadly game, and it can happen in a blink of an eye.

God doesn't give us trials and tribulations if he didn't think we couldn't handle it, and he knew I could handle this outcome because he knew what was on the other side of it, that it was a better door than the one I was in. He just needed to help push me out that door and into the next.

Revelation: *Random but take a sticky note and write on each one your favorite places to eat, put them in a hat, and pick one. That is where you need to go get food right now. I can't tell you how much "comfort" food has helped me get out of my head. Hibachi is usually my go-to place. What is yours?*

You're Fine, Everything Is Fine

When you're in your lane, there's no traffic.

Sitting here in bed, I think to myself, *How can I make this anxiety disorder completely go away?*

I guess it is simple, really. I can just type it all out like I am, and it'll be gone with a click of a button.

I beg to differ on that one, but really, you are going to be *just fine. I'm fine*, as I am saying it in my head like Ross Geller did in Friends.

I want to talk about a time I was at work, and I didn't think everything was fine. We have all probably had more than one moment at work where it felt like "I might lose my job with this one!" or "This could be the day I snap and quit!"

I worked at a place that had me working two different shifts, day turn and midnight about every other week. I thought it would be fine. I was young! But my body did not think it was fine or fun. I started to notice I was the only worker doing these shifts back and forth, and everyone else was set on one shift and going about their merry way, along with merry way to not working and just sitting there while I picked up all the slack, exhausted and wanting to catch up on sleep so badly, along with figuring out if Skittles was an appropriate meal. Eventually, after a year of this and hearing everyone complain about going to work, I decided to have a meeting with my manager to ask if, after a year, I proved myself to have one shift permanently like everyone else, and I didn't care which one because I wasn't a mom at the time.

Her response to me was "Who do you think you are asking if you proved yourself to have one shift when it has only been a year."

I honestly didn't even know how to respond to that comment when I asked so nicely with no attitude, no anger or animosity. Plus, I really am a hard worker and got tasks done, so I thought of why I wasn't deserving of having one shift. It was word vomit out of my mouth because right in that moment, I did have animosity right off my tongue. I know my face said it all, and I probably didn't even need to say anything, but I did.

Without thinking, I said, "You know, this is a really big problem for me, and it will be an even bigger one for you when I am gone and your lazy workers out there will have to actually pick up the slack like I have been."

During my midnight shift, I applied to a lot of jobs and got one in two weeks, closer to home. It all worked out for me in the end, and it didn't for her when she ended up getting fired after a few years.

I didn't like that I got to that point, but please, don't be like that manager. Just be kind to your employees and have an understanding heart, show the appreciation they deserve! That is why I am in HR, so I can be an advocate of kindness to the ones I currently work with. When they need help, I help them regardless of the circumstances!

This story just concludes that it is fine and it is okay to remove yourself from toxic places and people. I can't tell you how many toxic people I have removed from my life. Even though they weren't toxic to everyone or anyone else, they were toxic in mine, and God didn't want them placed in my circle anymore. Some people are easy to get rid of, and some, it was tough and emotional but needed to happen to get myself in a better alignment with the doors I was opening up. When you know, you know! I'm a very with-all-my-heart kind of person whether that is if I love you or, with all my heart, I need you to kindly step out of my lane.

Growing up, my mom always knew who was going to stay in my life and who wasn't. I thought, *How do you know these things? Are you a psychic? Can you predict the future? Are you Wonder Woman?* Nope, she was just *right* about everything. There isn't one person, place, or thing she was wrong about. I would sit there, venting to her via FaceTime, and she would say time and time again and to this very day, "I told you they weren't going to stay in your life!" Even though there were times I was sad about losing certain friends and even family members, I knew God could hear conversations I couldn't, and he silently took me away from anything he knew would hurt me, so I had to accept the process he was calling me into.

I was beginning to like being by myself. When Corey was working during the week, I was taking that time to reflect on myself, even on the days I didn't have Jaxx. I was finding that inner peace I so badly needed. Even when I didn't think I needed it, I absolutely did! I was going from can't get out of bed for two days to "Okay, this is really nice."

My two girls who never let me down are my mom and my childhood best friend, Alix. These two women are the definition of blessings. Not only are they selfless, but they are both wonderful moms and would do anything for anyone in need, including myself! There is nothing I can't tell them; they are honest, and they understand every circumstance. Alix knows every single thing about my life. She's a true sister, secret keeper, the friend who can bring up a memory and laugh about it like it happened yesterday, my hand holder through all and any pain I have been through, my mama twin because we had our firstborns three months apart. So we shared all the first-time pregnancy moments together. We graduated high school together and witnessed it all! We have stayed strong, building each other up, and I couldn't have asked for a better friend to share this life with.

Both reassure me constantly that I am fine, you are fine, we are all fine! I guess you only need a few awesome people in your life to help you close that window that's letting in the negativity. I love a small circle of people who are my true tribe. God makes it possible to have that in your life so don't take advantage of it. Don't get me wrong, I have other friends I love dearly, but these two are just my meat and potatoes, the peanut to my jelly, the brush to my paint! It is nothing personal to anyone else that I love!

Do you have someone you can lean on every day and maybe not even every day because let's be honest here, we are all busy and sometimes we don't have time for each other every second of the day.

It's the ones that make time for you when you need them the most that really count. Those are your people, don't let them go!

You aren't alone in this; you will be just fine on the journey you are walking in and called to. Don't let the mud on your boots take away the shine on those stilettos you have in your closet or those shiny business shoes for that important job you have been praying for. Always be ready for that storm to mess up that mascara or the gel in your hair, and remember you can always reapply it when the storm has passed and start anew. There is always a new chapter to begin, so keep writing and keep turning your pages.

> *You can never cross the ocean unless you have the courage to lose sight of the shore.* (Christopher Columbus)

Thoughts that repeat themselves are exhausting. The attack of the enemy will go on and on when you start believing in it, then you start to feel like you are being ambushed in the war you are in. Certain situations become unexpected, and we feel like we can't handle the battle we are in when we feel attacked. We are all challenged every day in our situations, trying to figure out our next move and how we can get unstuck because, of course, we don't want to stay there; we want to move. You need to reach and grab that hand reaching for you. He is going to lead you through the sea, through the rocks, through the attacks—he is the shield so you don't get stung. Depend on the hope right in front of you because I know that race was supposed to be forty miles, but now it has become eighty miles instead, and that is going to happen so just keep running through your race. There is always an ending to your victory run! Humble yourself and see the light so that, when you are being attacked, it can't and won't affect you, that you are strong enough to mentally push that attack away. Take your armor and get ready, stay alert.

"Cast all your anxiety on me," is all I hear when it hits and tries to take me out. I cast it all to him because that is all I know; it is all I've done all my life. I know my attacks are not as strong as what my heart can do and what he can do for me because he is not done with me yet. He is working through me for me.

What happens next after an anxiety attack? Will you let all your enemies win when you are in that battle? Will you let your thoughts drown? I always feel like someone is saying, "Take ten steps back, Jenni," but I scream back, "Nah, I'm going to take ten steps forward, watch me!" Talk positively out loud to yourself. Talk away and don't stop until those negative thoughts go away.

Revelation: *Who is the one person you lean on the most? Write their name/s on a sticky note and hang them up so you are reminded you are not alone because you always have them to help you open that new door coming your way. They are your saving grace in that gaslight!*

Rejection

You are not defined by your rejection.

Do you struggle with rejection in your life? Does it take control of something good right in front of you? If so, I understand that rejection can be a toxic entity that's hard to get away from.

Even when you really aren't being rejected, the feeling of the possibility of it is heart-wrenching; at least for me it is, knowing what it feels like. I dread the thought of it only because it has happened to me more than I can count, and I really do hate the feeling it brings. It's like a huge nauseating knot in your stomach every single time. A wave of emotions doubt and then the anxiety kicks in, and we all know the outcome of that.

Honestly, the reason I am bringing this to light is hopefully to help you get past the same things I suffer with, help you to get out of that funk that weighs you down, because you are more than rejection; we are all more than that! You see, the trauma in your life is what brings out the rejection because it is all you know, right? I have done a lot to help fix those thoughts out of my head, and some worked and some didn't. Depending on the situation at hand, you just need to know what is going to get you up off the ground and walk again.

Reading helps every negative aspect in my life, and I mean a page-turning, can't-get-myself-away-from-this-book kind. It takes me exactly where I need to be—out of my head, not thinking about that rejection.

Rejection comes in all kinds of forms. It could be a friend ghosted you, and you just have no idea why. You sit and think, *I wish I had closure on what I did wrong. Is it something I need to work on? Is it personal or not?* That one has been a hard one for me to let go of, but then I think, *It's not a Jenni issue. It's a "them issue."* You see, people come into our lives for a reason. Like a stepping stone to the next door you need to walk through, you don't get it now, but you will when it makes sense. I now look at this kind of rejection as a positive thing, where I needed that person in that moment, and now I no longer have space or time for them, and I am not anymore in theirs. Don't let it get to you like it sometimes does for me.

When you see that sketchy-looking door come up ahead that you know is the next one you have to walk through, go in positive knowing it won't be the first or the last. Looks can be deceiving. To the game-changing door in your next chapter, you won't know that until you walk through it.

Family rejection is the hardest one to swallow, and this is an emotional roller coaster that I deal with currently and what stings the worst. I just want to put it out there that family is everything, but sometimes it's the one thing that will break you in half when it hurts. I've held onto things way too much and have gotten extremely upset over what has been a nightmare, and lately it is something I have learned to let go of. It is not worth it; it is not worth trying to fix what is broken. Moving on is the best medicine in this scenario. As badly as it sucks to put that out there, it just really is the only way. Give it all to God, and he will be sure to make it right in the right time. Sometimes the enemy tries to take the context out of your relationships with family and friends and violate the contract you have with God to set your story straight, so remember to keep everything in context and keep it moving. Don't let the rejection win this term and season of your journey.

Nobody should have to prove themselves to anyone, especially family. The one rule I have said to myself is family should be the first constant in your life, the ones that would give everything to be there and hold you when times are hard. Truth is, that is not what happens at all. And I am not saying all family members, just the ones who may be a little lost in their own world, so we need to give them grace and pray they come back from whatever it is that is bogging them down or even someone that changes them into someone they aren't. I put faith in that God is working on them just as much as me, so step away and let him work. It is not our place to disturb.

Let rejection teach you a valuable lesson. Don't go back to what rejects you. Don't be the one rejecting and not giving that person the closure they deserve. Don't let that rejection define who you are inside. Don't let rejection turn you into a bitter mess. You are better than all of that. Instead, be grateful that rejection came at the time that it did, or things could be different for you. We should understand that rejection happens for a reason at the time God needs it to happen, so he can continue to work on the next move he has planned for you.

I am learning to understand this myself. I know it isn't easy, and it's not something you can just forget about right then right now. Some things, depending on what happened to you, will take time to heal and process to get over it, which nearly killed you mentally, so don't let anything else get in the way of your happiness. Take it with a grain of salt and a lesson learned.

You shine bright even when you feel lost. Always remember you are a light for someone else who needs it! Don't be their rejection. Be their guide, make a difference, and take your pain to make it easier on someone who needs it today. It just might make you feel whole again or save a life.

> *All things work together for good.* (2 Corinthians 9:8)

Revelation: *Take a sticky note and write the worst rejection you've ever been through. Now rip it up, burn it, shred it, stomp on it, whatever you need to do to release it, and forget about it. That's not your life anymore!*

It Happens Sometimes

We can't help everyone, but everyone can help someone.

—Ronald Reagan

We have times when we want to be alone and times when we dread being alone. Isolation is good for you, but sometimes it's the worst, and you just need to find the balance to know when the right time to be by yourself is and the right time when you need someone to talk to and get through this battle you're fighting. We shouldn't have to battle anything alone, and we aren't.

It could be music, a book, a walk, or even the same series you've watched ten times now; for me that's *Friends, New Girl,* and the *X-Files*! Then there are times when I need to call my mom and not be alone, so I can talk to her or Corey to get out of isolation when I am by myself. I have even found times when I stayed at work in my office, so I was around my coworkers and wasn't ready to go home and isolate myself. It is all on how you are feeling in that moment.

I am a talker. Anyone who knows me and has had conversations with me knows I don't shut up sometimes. I have had people tell me I talk a lot and ramble on, and sometimes I can tell by their face that they want me to stop talking. I hate that feeling when I know this and even when it is told to me. I am here to tell you why I am this way, and maybe you are the same kind of person and understand where I am coming from.

I am alone most of the time, and most of my life, I've spent talking to myself, to an animal I know is listening but can't talk back, along with a little one who also has struggled with years of no communication so, technically, talking to a child who has no idea what

I am saying. Then there is my prayer jar and talking and praying through anything and everything to move past being alone. When I finally am able or have any kind of conversation with a person who can understand me, can maybe console me in the situation, I begin to go on a rant or vent session. Sometimes it's just a casual talk to engage in any human interaction except for my overstimulated subconscious mind! I don't even realize I ramble. I just let it out. I think it's an anxiety thing I have; anxiety just kind of takes over, and I want so badly to just gravitate with that person.

When I met Corey for the first time, I remember thinking, *Wow, he talks just as much as me, if not more!* I was really excited about that because I longed for someone to be on the same level as me so we can always have a conversation and it never runs dry, and it doesn't. Loneliness was a true thing before I met him, so I had a lot of talking and catching up to do that I wanted to tell a human being about, a daily best friend!

He said in a text when we first met, "If I am talking too much, just please tell me to shush!"

I laughed, thinking, *No way! Keep going!*

Three years later, we are still going! Now he tells me I talk a lot. Let's not state the obvious here.

Working in human resource, I work with a lot of people and personalities in all different departments and good people at that, right in the heart of Youngstown in blue collar. I love when someone comes into my office and engages in really anything. Don't get me wrong, I work in a busy atmosphere, so sometimes I don't want to be bothered so I can get a project done in time. But when that employee comes in with a problem they are facing, it can be easy for me to shut off that light bulb I have going on and revert to a new one with that employee who needs me. Even when I have a pile of deadlines to get to, I always make them my priority, and I love putting them first. They trust me to be there for them, and that's a good feeling to have. Anyone that works in human resource knows people be peopling—that's a good saying I heard from the HR Besties Podcast that Leigh Henderson, Ashley Herd, and Jamie Jackson said that has stuck with me and a true fact at that. And we get a lot of the personalities out there, but I love it because everyone deserves to be *heard*, even if it is something they need to work on. Who isn't a work in progress, right? And in human resources, it's our job to be there to help them prosper and mold them into where they want to go in life, whether that's a growth aspect in their career or pushing them into education we can help with to grow elsewhere. I am always honored to be able to help someone in need when it comes to growing within their career. At Hynes, it's not a job; it's a career! Happiness is the key, and we want you to love the job you are in! I mean, come on, we spend most of our time working anyways; we might as well love it, and I sure do love mine.

I wanted to title this chapter, "It Happens Sometimes," because I think and say this all the time when the unexpected falls into my lap. It's my way of being "positive," like, "Aah, it happens, let's move on, Jenni!" That part of my five minutes, hour, day, month, year is over; onto the next one.

I never used to think this way in the past, but motherhood has challenged me in ways I never thought I could be challenged on. So I look at things in a different light because as Jaxx grows older, new things will sprout, and I will say, *"It happens.* Now let's figure this out and learn from it because it won't be the end of the world." I know something bigger will spring up on me when I least expect it, so I might as well move on and let it be.

I know my mother's out there; I understand this all too well. For good reasons though, we have growing babies who are learning how to process everything in the world, and it is our job to teach and lead them to know how to calm the emotions they don't understand.

I am thirty-four years old and is still trying to figure out new emotions I've never experienced before. That will never change for any of us. There is no end point to the age when we will stop growing our minds and trying to surface that progress. Emotions are never ending until the day we die, so get on that roller coaster and enjoy the ride.

Are you an introvert or extrovert? Is it easy for you to start a conversation? Are you shy and barely talk in fear of not knowing what to say, or are you afraid you might say the wrong thing?

It's all okay either way. That is a part of your personality and how you deal with whatever you are battling. Some of us need to get it all out, maybe even scream a little. Some talk to someone like they are yelling at them, but really, they are just yelling out loud about the story to get the aggression out. Then they feel better. I know I've done that and stopped midsentence after looking at their reaction and have to say, "I am not yelling at you, just venting to you." After you say that, then they completely get it. Kind of like a been-there-done-that scenario.

I hope you understand all your "it happens" moments because it really does just happen for all of us. There is no pressure to dig deep into something we can try and find our way out of. Even if it takes a minute, it will release itself. Trust the process of what God is doing for you, and then you will be glad it started the way that it did.

Revelation: *Write down your biggest blowup moment with a family or friend, maybe even a coworker, and how did you handle it afterward? What made you say, "It happens"?*

Mud

If you can't stop thinking about it, don't stop working on it.

I had a vision while driving to work one day. It was raining pretty hard, and I was dropping Jaxx off to school. He and I had a rough morning of him being frustrated and me trying to understand what the problem was, being his communication skills are a little on the edgy side.

I kept saying out loud, "Lord, what is the issue here? Help me understand to make this easier for both of us."

I didn't think I was going to get a response that quickly. In less than thirty minutes of my drive, I had a vision of myself and Jaxx together in rain boots. I didn't want to run in the mud or the rain, but he did naturally. Pulling and tugging at my hand to "Come on, Mom! Let's play," I did it and he was able to run through the mud gracefully while I struggled and could not get out of it for the life of me. Jaxx came back, and as the sweet little boy that he is, he tried helping me out of the mess.

I said, "I can't do it, Jaxx, I'm stuck."

Those little hands got me right out like he was a miracle worker, and off we went into the rain!

I took that sign as God was Jaxx in that moment, and I was asking for help, so he came over to help me when I felt stuck in it. He was telling me there was nothing I couldn't do to help me get through even muddy waters, valleys, mountaintops, and so much more. "Trust in me and I will lead you!" I thought it was so powerful that he used Jaxx, the innocence of him and the fact that the reason I was frustrated was because of him. He was teaching me how to be patient in the moments that I can't grasp and surrender it all to him. I also took it as he has a good hand on Jaxx and his future, that I should not worry that he will go down a bad path or road in his life—God will guide him through that rain and mud. And he showed me that he can absolutely go through it with no problems, but I couldn't catch up without the help of those little hands.

Do you ever feel like you are failing? Almost like being stuck in that mud repeatedly? Just remember you are not a failure in life, but understand we have to fail at things to rise from it, learn above it, and see fit we know how to fight it. You are beyond any failure your path brings your way. That storm will pass, and God will be your lifeguard.

Nobody knows the amount of tears you've cried except for God. He knows and feels all the pain you are feeling. Don't be discouraged and know he is fighting this battle with you. He doesn't want to see you fail just as much as you don't want to be in it.

The ultimate vision

To get off the topic of mud, I have an even better vision that looks a little prettier and one that I get back all the time.

It started right before I met Corey in 2021. I was struggling the most personally on myself—I didn't think I would ever find anyone who would love me unconditionally, and I didn't want to meet anyone in fear I would be right back to square one, and that was a paralyzing fear that left me motionless. God had bigger plans, and he knew the only way to get me out of that headspace was to not give me a dream while I was sleeping but a vision so beautiful, it would be impossible to forget. He also made sure that wasn't an option to forget since he gives it back to me tenfold time and time again!

It was the beginning of summer in 2021. I woke up feeling anxious with my divorce about to be final in less than a month. I was emotional and couldn't stop crying. I wanted some kind of sign to know the journey ahead was going to be more comfortable and improved. While I was getting ready for work, I had a vision of myself on the beach, and of all the places I thought, why the beach? I'm a mountain girl along with having a horrible *fear* of the ocean.

But he gave it to me, and I proceeded to let the vision play out with no questions asked.

The sun was rising, and it was the perfect view of the sky with orange tones all around me. I was wearing a white dress in all silk, and my hair was long and wavy like I just got out of the salt water and let it dry. The air was calm, and there were no waves, just silence. No birds, no human existence, nothing but me and that wide-open ocean space. Until it opened…it was so beautiful as the rising sun was shining through, and all around me was that water. I creeped up closer, but I started to fear walking through, that the water would crash down on me.

I said, "Lord, I can't walk through this! I am not ready, and I am scared!"

He whispered in my ear, "My child, there is no reason to fear for I am with you always, and I have plans for you, good things that will bring you joy and help you prosper. Trust in me and let me carry you to those first steps!"

I was crying as I was typing this.

The next moment in that vision, I heard Jaxx's voice running to me as he greeted me with that amazing smile he has. He latched on and held my hand so tight and pointed to the opening of the sea, excited to venture through it.

But I stopped him and said, "I am not ready!"

Then a man approached me, and I could not see his face. I was not scared, and I did not back off—I let him come closer and grab my hand and look straight ahead with me as he leaned in closer to show I was safe.

God said, "Take that first, stepchild. It is the only path I have for you, and it is one you will find your peace."

I took one step and stopped, and the vision was gone.

A month later, Corey came into my life, and I was convinced that man was him, knowing what I know now, and the man that he is, God prepared me for him stepping into my life at the most challenging wake of my world. He knew Corey would see those broken pieces I had and helped me put them back together, and he has done just that and more! There was no judgement, and it was exactly who

I needed in my life. God created every timing in mine and his life for this. The whole time I was questioning my life and every move I made, and here was God, working behind the scenes for that very moment. I was always his, and he was always mine, and we just didn't know it yet.

I still get that vision when God knows I need it most, and he brings it to me to show me the steps I have and am making in the open sea to that light. I am not quite at the end of it in fear of the ocean, but with baby steps and every journey I embark on currently, God is carrying me closer to what is more *yeses* in my life and even more *amens!*

> *Guard your heart above all else, for it determines the course of your life.* (Proverbs 4:23)

"Oceans (Where Feet May Fail)" by Hillsong is my anthem after this vision. It speaks to me on so many levels to connect how I was and still do feel about the vision he gave me during such a vulnerable time in my life. If you have never listened to it, I recommend it to help you get through the vulnerable state you may currently be in.

What you are going through, whether that is the muddy valley or the open seas, is valuable and not taken lightly. I promise you, I know that whatever seems small to someone else is big for you, and I validate whatever your storm is.

If you are battling a chronic illness, grieving a loved one, lost your job, going through a divorce, miscarriage, mental health problems, financial issues, battling identity, lost your home, loneliness, depression, abandonment, grieving an animal, taking care of a sick loved one, overwhelmed, or suicidal thoughts—all these and many more are validated in my book, and you have room in my circle and most importantly his! Have a seat. Let's talk!

Revelation: *What is your favorite book? Any genre is fine, I just want you to go to that place or dive into those words that can take you away from whatever is toxic in your life, what helps you get out of your current situation into a different mindset! Write that book on your sticky note and go back to that page or chapter that helps you the most! Let God carry you to that place.*

2024

You don't have to be perfect to be amazing.

As the new year is approaching fast, I am realizing that 2023 was just not the best, but it was also not the worst either.

I had major falling outs with family in 2023 with a lot unknown to things and silent treatments that were leaving me anxious, bothered, sad, angry, confused, sleepless. To this day, there are still unanswered questions, and I will either get the understanding message later on or never. I am just putting faith in God that this is just something he has allowed me to surrender it all to him.

I suffered battles with Jaxx and is coming to terms that he may have a spectrum of autism, or some ADHD. The reality of that hit me hard on the month of October. As it started to mentally drain me with questions and doubts, I was having a hard time focusing on things at work and even at home. *How will his future look? Can I get him the help he needs in time? Will people stop looking at him weird when they don't understand why he acts a certain way or asking why he covers his ears when something isn't loud but to him it bothers him?* These are just a few things that have been on my mind, but I am determined that 2024 is going to be the biggest year of growth for him as help is lingering closer, for not only Jaxx but for myself and my family to know how to understand what we need to do to help support him with any curveballs he may come across. I promise I will always be a shield to any obstacle he comes across. Even if I don't know exactly what to do at that moment, I will figure it out. It doesn't go without saying that any fear Jaxx may come across, I will be sure to shield him from all and any of it. But I also know not all battles are for me to handle.

I have left places and cried the whole way home or dreaded going anywhere in fear that I will be stuck in a situation, leaving me anxious over Jaxx and others around me. Some weekends left me in limbo, and I would gravitate to Corey, asking, "What do I do? I'm stuck!" Thank goodness for him because, most of the time, he knows what to say at just the right time so we can figure it out together. Not knowing what to do is sometimes normal as a parent, and it gives comfort that others struggle just as much as you, if not more. I just know watching your son struggle with things other kids do so well and knowing he needs that push or special treatment can be beyond challenging, especially when certain people in the system fail to help you, knowing that is your only outlet. Holly Furtick said in one of her sermons that we need to stop comparing ourselves to other moms, along with god telling her god gave her this child because you have what they need. That hit me like a strong wave and gave me peace that I am never alone and I am what Jaxx needs. God knew Jaxx needs my light, and what other people do so well doesn't mean I am not doing well either. I also need to thank Bobbi Kaleel for always telling me time and time again that I am the best mom; sometimes you just need those words. I want to pay that forward and tell all the moms out there that you are amazing and the best mom to your babies every day of their lives! I came to terms that the system was not my only outlet, and I needed to give it all to God to come to terms on his endgame with finding peace of mind. I stopped worrying so much over his actions and started praying through it, and it got me exactly to where I needed Jaxx to be at!

Recently, this is something I have let go of because while Jaxx is getting the help he needs and I am doing everything in my heart to give him what he needs to blossom into the man I know he can be, to succeed and prosper means I have to let go and let God do the work for him. There are no therapists in the world that are going to help him like he will. Faith goes a long way when you feel a little doubt.

Jaxx is also not defined by his struggles or by anyone who wants nothing to do with him, who doesn't know him, or doesn't come around or involve their life in his, and that's okay; it really is! He has so many wonderful family and friends who love him and support his journey because, at the end of the day, God controls his life and what and who needs to be in it like he does for all of us. There may come a time in his life when he will ask me questions on why this happened and why his current state is happening, so I want to have all the preparation to help guide him in the door he will be walking through, knowing God will be the true leader, but I can be the advocate to help push him in the right direction.

In 2023, I made a decision that was a big one for my future but also for my health. I had a medical situation that ultimately put me on the next journey of never being able to have children ever again. It was emotional for months before. Afterward, I would wake up seeing my mom's face, thinking, *I will never experience pregnancy or holding my own little child in my arms ever again, it's done!* Without going into details on what was happening, I just knew it was the best long-term choice for me. I was in a lot of pain constantly, and it put a lot of strain on my daily life. My doctor also knew it was best for my future. Ever since that surgery, I have felt amazing internally and externally, and I know Corey and everyone else who knows what I was going through knows that it really put a brighter light on my life mentally.

I'd be lying if I didn't have moments of sadness when I see babies or when I am cleaning Jaxx's room and go through all his baby stuff I still keep, so I can look at from time to time, reminisce on those baby smells I miss so much. But the positive part about it is I get to love my family and friends' little ones and make an impact on their lives just as much as Jaxx's, so I am not missing out on those memories.

Corey and I love the life we have with Jaxx and our little family together, so in the end, it turned out to be okay! God knew I needed to be a mama but knew in due time, soon, I was not going to be able to be one, and my clock was ticking. So he said, "This needs to happen now," so Jaxx could be the guiding light I badly needed to the storm before God let Corey enter my life. Isn't that wild? I think that is so powerful. I would have never thought in a million years that I would be having a life-changing surgery that would stop me from having another child and that Jaxx would be it. I anticipated having one more baby, but God said no and made it okay for me! He turned my storm into a rainbow!

God takes ahold of that valley and knows all the highs and lows; he knows how to take it slow if that's what we need, and he knows how to speed it up when it starts getting risky. We have no reason to question anything. Even if we rotate and turn to him, he will help you surrender it all.

There are situations when I surrender everything, and then I question, "Why did I surrender something when I see no change happening?" and "Why do I still feel horrible inside? Isn't he supposed to help me?" I would sometimes do feel really bad for even feeling that way, knowing he moves all the mountains for me so I can walk all the valleys. He opens all those doors and closes the ones that are no good anymore, so I can get to the next. He lights that candle, so I can find my way and don't get lost. And when I think I am alone, I am never. I was feeling selfish thinking all the negative things and the "I want it now, Lord!" But he never judged me once for feeling that way; he just gave me signs to stay humble and silent in his work.

If you have gone through this or are currently struggling with it, it is going to be okay! When you see that valley ahead and become scared, just go—walk that valley and know, when you have doubts, God isn't doubting at all. He knows exactly what is ahead for all of us, and he's excited for the reaction you will have when you get to the end. Find that light and reach, don't quit! You might have to go through some mud or a storm, but what doesn't kill you makes you stronger.

I've had many years that made me strong, but 2023 was a different kind of strength; every year will be a different battle that you will define as your strength, your battle cry.

I learned how to back off when I was angry and hurt, and normally I am not the one to do that. I speak up and usually say things I don't mean, and I did some of that a few times in 2023, but then I felt like God needed me to lie low and not focus on the things that was not worth focusing on. He was giving me signs to let him handle the background while I continued to focus on my current path so I can walk into 2024 with the high hopes of knowing God will handle what is ahead of me without me trying to shift gears. He needed me to understand that there is a reason we have rearview mirrors and why, when we keep pressing on, they start to fade away.

Do you have a valley you are having a hard time focusing on? Is the path God has led you on looking blurry and weak? If so, don't give up, keep that candle lit, and have faith he will keep it bright for you. If you think that light is dimming, he will find a way to bring it back, so you can get through the valleys to your mountains. Keep your faith strong!

Revelation: *What is the main goal you prayed for in 2023 that you wanted to see in 2024? Did you complete it? Still working on it? Write on a sticky what that is and keep your heart focused on what God can and will do for you in the years to come, and when it happens for you, you can keep it close to your heart!*

Mason Jars

Growth is painful, change is painful, but there is nothing
as painful as staying stuck somewhere you don't belong.

Can you imagine every thought, fear, dream, fantasy, laughter, story was all locked up in a mason jar? Can you even fathom the amount we would have? I think about what my massive room would look like with all the mason jars glowing to the point that a lamp wouldn't be needed to fixate on what is around me. My room would be tainted with beautiful flowers that never die, pictures framed all around with all my loved ones, and don't forget all my sticky notes; those are coming with me! Nothing would ever be lost because every jar was filled with something that made me feel alive. Even if it hurt me, it made sure to let me know I was alive and conquered it.

I would never have to explain myself because every jar was a story of its own. I hope when my time comes, and I am greeted in the gates of heaven, I am taken to something similar or exactly this. I believe every dream and prayer is locked away, and it is never forgotten, showing us all prayers are listened to and accepted.

I imagine what heaven looks like all the time. Not that I want to be there right now, but I'm not afraid of what is to come for me, especially if I do have a roomful of mason jars waiting for me with dragonflies all around on a mountain, a perfect sunset or sunrise with the most beautiful orange ray of lighting around the clouds. Now that is a perfect view in my eyes.

When Corey and I go on our bike trips, I take at least fifty to one hundred pictures per trip of all the views and skies. There is just something about clouds and that ray of sunshine peeping through that gets me in all the feels, almost like God is telling me a story while I am basking in all his beauty around me, taking it all in with the man of my dreams. Family is always saying, "Jenni and those clouds she loves…" They probably think I am nuts taking cloud photo after cloud photo, and to them, they probably all look the same, but they don't to me. I am just blessed enough God gave me a man who loves the views just as much as I do, and it is something we can make memories with together because, before I met him, I did none of this. I was never with anyone who was even remotely close to wanting to walk out of the house to do the things Corey and I do now. And now I have Jaxx, loving the clouds and the skies. "Look, Mommy, the sky!" he would say.

I want every traveling experience to be in my mason jars, from the Smoky Mountains; Nashville; Pikes Peak; Mount Evans; Aspen; Michigan; Salem, Massachusetts; Sturgis; Badlands; Garden of the Gods; Iowa; South Dakota; Pennsylvania; and so much more that I have traveled to on the bike with him, through the sun, rain, hail, and wind. Lock those mason jars up because they have all been, and always will be, good memories I want and will cherish the rest of my life, for the once-in-a-lifetime opportunity I was able to see and continue to see.

When we went on a random bike ride in April, we had no idea where the GPS was taking us; we just knew it was windy roads and the weather was gorgeous. We didn't care.

He kept saying, "I have no idea where we are at or where we are going!"

I said, "That's the fun of the unknown."

While he said, "It's unknown all right."

I laughed and thought the fun of the unknown can be so beautiful. An unknown memory trapped in a mason jar is all I see while going around those bends, enjoying all of God's life around us!

I hope you learn to let go and let God

We say we need to crawl before we can walk and that every lesson is like crawling for the first time. I was getting ready one morning, and I thought, *Wait, we technically don't crawl first. We have to hold our heads up, roll over to then get in the position to crawl, get the strength to lift our bodies up, and hold onto something to then learn to let go and then start taking those steps to walk.* As we become toddlers, we do a lot of running so our parents can panic to grab us before we get into something we shouldn't, and as adults to this day, we are still learning how to lean on things to help us walk into new chapters of our lives, like leaning on our moms to help us become moms ourselves, leaning on that new recipe book so we don't fail at our first casserole for a picnic, leaning on our dads to show us how to change that tire when and if we get a flat on the road, leaning on our grandparents to help us with those words of wisdom we so dearly need sometimes to shape us up when we need it, to keep us humble. You see, we are always going to be learning how to crawl again and leaning on that object or person; we are all always a work in progress to the next crawl before the steps.

I hope your mason jars show you all the steps you have taken and all the battles to the victories you conquered.

Fireflies

Do any of you remember taking mason jars out in the middle of camping by a lake, in the woods, in your backyard, at the park and capturing those fireflies? I have such a vivid memory of doing this when I was a little girl. They were always out, and I was always catching them and making my mason jars light up but only temporarily because I didn't want them to die. So I captured them for a moment and released them to freedom. Now I seriously never see them anymore. It is like they don't exist in our world now. I thought how cool they looked in the night sky, glowing up. I imagined them as little silent angels flying around, guiding us to the light we need. They made me so happy, and I miss seeing them. I may be crazy, but I really haven't seen them since I was a child. Am I alone in this?

I can't be the only one who did this—glowing up whatever object we had in our hands and for me the mason jars! What did you use?

Look at your life as a firefly in the night; you are lighting up the world with your bright smile. Even if you don't think you have a light to give, you absolutely do—God shines all those rays so you can walk through the shadows. How else do you think you are going to walk in the valleys without it? He makes it happen for you and everyone around you; you all have the light of a thousand journeys. I know if I have to learn to crawl again, I am crawling with the light he is giving me, so I can lean on what I need to get back up to walk again, so I can get to that new door straight ahead because I am eager to see what is behind it…aren't you?

I have faith in all that you are doing and going to do. When we all get to those gates in heaven one day, I can't wait to visit your room of mason jars, so we can share our stories together for eternity. I am not afraid of what God has in store for me, and you shouldn't be either!

Revelation: *Write on a sticky note the most treasured mason jar memory and why it is so special and dear to your heart. Keep it safe and hold it close. That is going to be your constant to keep you going!*

Monster under the Bed

He drew me up from the pit of destruction, out of the miry bog, and set my feet upon a rock, making my steps secure.

—Psalm 40:2 ESV

The summer of seventh grade changed my life, in many ways than just one. The start of my parents' divorce, being sexually molested, the take-your-breath-away anxiety, and the doubled-over depression hit my world in a spin.

I have gone back to this chapter too many times to count and have contemplated even putting the pages in, but I know someone somewhere needs to have hope that they can get through the very thing I once did, so this is the most vulnerable one and the most emotional thing I have written about.

Let's back up to sixth grade real quick and set it to September 11, the day that changed all our lives. After that day, a lot spiraled in the world, including mine. I didn't understand why the towers came down, and I didn't understand that it would give me a floodgate of tears when I got older, once I understood the impact it had on not only the world but the families involved. All I thought sitting in my math class was *Wow this looks awful and scary, but I have no idea what is going on.* My mom picked my brother and I up, and I just remember watching my family glued to the news all day on the updates conspiring. It was a changed world for all of us.

Singing was a huge part of my life, starting in fifth or sixth grade, and my family was just introduced to it with me. It wasn't just a good voice God graced me with that I didn't know I had, but it was my escape from reality. That's all I really cared about. Throughout my school years, starting from sixth grade, I was singing solos in the choir, the National Anthem for school sports and events, I sang for the Phantom Hockey games, tried out for *American Idol* the summer going into my senior year, the Scrappers baseball game in my early twenties, and many karaoke contests. On my senior year, I got the lead role in our first musical, *Grease*, where I got to play Sandy. I was loving all of it, and music was what made me feel like there was a constant in my life.

I was excited to start seventh grade mainly because I worked hard to get on the volleyball team, and I was excited to start something new and exciting. Conditioning over the summer was intense and fun, along with making new friends and distracting myself from my parents arguing about their divorce and all the changes that came with it all when your parents split. But nothing was really the same once I started seventh grade; it changed my life forever.

Remember when I told you sometimes family can break your heart? Well, here it comes! I was sexually molested by a family member going into my seventh grade year, and to say it's easy to forget is nonexistent; you just learn to cope. That alone is still not easy and never will be. The one thing that kills me inside every time is that he took my innocence away from me when I didn't want that to happen. I was scared. I was young. I was lost. It is why I jump every time someone creeps on me and I become paranoid at anything that deals with something like this; even movies or shows on TV make me extremely emotional when it pertains to watching someone get touched or hurt in any way without consent.

God is what stood by me on those scary nights to let me know I was going to be okay when nobody else understood or even tried to. He was and still is the monster under my bed. That will never go away, so I lean on God to take that pain away for me because nothing in my way will be able to help me through that except for him. I have learned that God protects me when I am afraid because he wants me to trust him and to not be afraid.

So do not be afraid of them, for there is nothing concealed that will not be, disclosed, or hidden that will not be made known. (Matthew 10:26)

*You will not have to fight this battle. Take up
your positions; stand firm and see the deliverance
the Lord will give you.* (2 Chronicles 20:17)

With everything already going on in my life and being frightened 24-7, I just didn't know what to do, but to think as a young girl to move past it and not upset my family or give them something to stress about since they already had enough on their plate, and I should be the last person to add even more stress, I know now that thinking this was a bad idea. I should have done something right away. It wouldn't have taken the pain away, but it would have saved me some late-night crying sessions with myself, and I could have been able to talk to someone sooner, instead of creating a rabbit hole for myself. I kept this in for two years and let this monster walk around like it was okay, when really all I thought about was all the horrible things I wanted to happen to him after the pain he inflicted on me.

I had a lot of friends in seventh and/or eighth grade, and going into my freshman year, even with this haunting secret I kept inside of me, I couldn't hold it in much longer, and it came out like vomit when I was on the phone with my gram while my dad was in the living room. I was a pretty angry person those past two years with everyone at the start of this, so I had enough of it all and just spilled the beans about what happened to me, hung up the phone, looked at my dad's face as it turned into pure terror, while he called my mom to come over as soon as possible to discuss what was going on. Since they were divorced, they had to put what they went through together aside to get to the bottom of what was happening and why I didn't say anything right away. My friends, Jenni tends to think more about others than she does herself; that is the true verdict on that. Of course, they believed every word I said and made me go to counseling, which was not helping at all, especially when my counselor made my last session like a conference call but in *person*! Yes, I said it, in person with this monster and his parents, who didn't believe a word I said. I can recall his shirt saying, "I have issues," during this "meeting." Counseling sessions were over for me up until now; it took me nineteen years to really trust the process of trusting an outside person with my life.

I was even angrier and bitter after that. He went to the same school as me, which didn't make it any better with the fact that he was "family" to begin with. He went around admitting what he did to me to the whole school and that I allowed it, which traumatized me to no end, that someone who did something so awful would admit to my school that he was proud of it and lie that I allowed this horrible thing to happen to me. Instead of the friends I had asking if I was okay and if I needed to talk about it, they all pushed me away, thought I was gross, and didn't want to be my friend anymore, so my social life was out the door for a while! Not only was going home for me wrecking my world with my dad's drinking getting worse with his girlfriend at the time, not seeing my mom as much due to work, but going to school was an anxiety attack every morning because I hated everyone around me, even with volleyball because a lot of my so-called friends played this sport with me. So I eventually stopped playing volleyball after my fourth year. I was beginning to feel like a complete loner and loser at this point.

The worst was after my family knew what happened, they still allowed this monster to come to family social events (talk about punching me in the stomach). Thankfully, they got the hint, and he stopped coming around. I thought, *Why even try to let him come around? Did it not sink in the first time on what I said he did to me? Did you not believe me? Why would I lie about something like that?* Only my parents and brother were there for me; none of my other family even sat down with me to talk and help me through the trauma I was experiencing. I felt like they also thought I was lying. It was extremely hurtful, and it has taken me a long time to trust family members in my life, especially if it could have been my safety. To me, they didn't care.

I prayed through this. I prayed so hard that I thought my prayer jar was going to overflow over and over again. I just wanted God to scoop me up and take me away. But he never left; he protected me this whole time, and he was the only constant in my life. He made sure I was not alone at night.

I spiraled after I was out of high school with my drinking, not respecting myself, my relationships, my family. I went down a dark door I didn't see myself getting out of. I had disrespect happen repeatedly that made me lose even more faith in my family and everyone else around me. It was to the point where I was not trusting anything or anyone, especially my dad when he disowned me as his daughter in his drunken escapade going against me to the cops with his girlfriend who physically attacked me. We didn't speak for a solid year. The disowning and rejection of not protecting me made my drinking out of control. It made my depression deafening, made me think things I shouldn't have been thinking, the past would flood in, and I would cripple in fear of certain things happening again. I knew it needed to stop at some point because I just wasn't feeling good, not only externally but mentally. This mentality was not a good look on me! I still had the faith of the Lord by my side, and I was and am completely grateful for him for all of it, for all the nos he gave me when I wanted a *yes*.

These battles made me so strong. Even when I thought I couldn't and wouldn't be strong enough to get through the storms, I had God to carry me. There was nothing he couldn't do to improve my life. He knew the path he had for me was going to wake me up to my *bigger* purpose. I said, "Let's go," and that's exactly what happened next.

Do you want to get well? (John 5:6)

I wanted to feel well. I knew depression was always creeping in and out of my life. I was battling what didn't make sense all the time. I was feeling stuck when it hit and when hope was fading. I was in a relationship with a man I was about to marry, and it was like God was pulling at me to not give up. He was taking me further into the eye of the storm. It was going to cost me a lot, and it did, but he made the hope in my heart wider, rejoice louder, rise higher! He made me live again even during the hardest battle of my life. He made me ready even when I didn't see it coming.

Revelation: *He will never leave you, nor forsake you in the middle. Feed off his faithfulness and surrender everything to him. Place on your sticky note your darkest fears and then write how you are going to get rid of that fear.*

Devil at My Table

All the forces of darkness cannot stop what God has ordained.

—Isaiah 14:27

I danced with the devil, I slept with the devil, and he sat at my table in multiple seats. Scary but that was my life for a while, and I was blind to it. He manipulated me, ripped my heart out and tore it into pieces, then smiled at me and did it again at my most fragile moments. I gave him the benefit of the doubt and thought I could save him. But God said, "It's not your job to save him, it's mine!" So I did the tango with him for a while until God said, "That's enough, child…" as he picked me up and took me to my new door, my new season.

So here I am, and here's my story of how I found victory during a very hard storm, the hardest storm out of all the chapters in my life. This door needed to shut and should have shut a long time ago, but God had other plans for me so I could get to where I am today! I am strong enough now to understand everything he did for me was for the good of my future ahead.

Blindsided by the time Jaxx turned two and found out my ex was being unfaithful our whole relationship for six years, I know I had a different monster under my current bed at the time, and I was fixed to remove myself, along with finding out my closest family knew what was happening a month before my wedding. They watched me walk down that aisle knowing the monster I was about to say, "*I do,*" to was a cold-hearted man about to crush my soul. They thought I wouldn't understand or believe something so close to the big day but in reality, after hearing what was going on I would have absolutely listened and walked away. As hard as it still is knowing they let this happen, I learned to forgive them because I wouldn't have Jaxx with also the promise they would never do this to me again, I put grace in my heart for my family even though it left me damaged.

Some probably thought it was easy to leave, and it was and was not; it was not because we had a little child together, and I put faith in the relationship. It was easy because I have more respect for myself then and now than I ever did in the past; especially with being a new mom, I knew the only way to move past low self-esteem was to get out and start anew to the woman I know I need to be for myself and my little boy. It obviously came with the baggage of no self-worth at all, the worst anxiety I have ever experienced in my life, tears, anger, resentment, illness, weight loss, abandonment within myself, doctors' appointments, friendships lost, family. But at the end of it all, I knew how and what to use to find myself again with the strength of my faith and my son. I knew it was all possible with that; I needed nothing else.

I moved beyond all of it because it is amazing what a healthy relationship can do for a toxic one—it completely erases the pain. The only hard part about a healthy relationship is trying not to bring in any past toxic triggers. I can't say both of us have not brought that in, but we communicate through it and reassure each other we are both better than the past we both endured, and we are better together because of it. That makes for a very happy and bright future for us both.

She held the world together because she knew
what it felt like to be in pieces. (Gemma Troy)

The only way out is through. I went through the longest stride of my life and came out on top. They say going through a divorce is like grieving a person long gone, but I looked at it like I was grieving myself and not that person I lost because, to be honest, I was happy it was long gone. But I lost a part of my soul I was trying to get back.

When I found out the news of what six years of my life was going on and all the details, I can honestly say I sat there and watched my soul leave out of my body while looking at myself in complete and utter confusion. Why did I not see this coming? What was I doing to not see the signs? Am I dumb? Am I a fool? Did I deserve this? Am I being punished? I could not get those questions out of my head. I was not eating or sleeping because I was finding a new place to live and starting over along with working a full-time job to keep providing for Jaxx. At one point, I didn't even want explanations as to why things happened the way that they did because I was moving on to better things, and I needed to solely focus on that to not feel crazy in my head. They just seemed to make things worse knowing all the details.

Then you will know the truth and the truth will set you free. (John 8:32)

It took years and time to finally not feel angry anymore, and only one person got me out of that mindset real fast with his words of wisdom: Corey! He told me while I was venting to him in the garage on something and anything that was upsetting me with my ex, with our shared parenting that sometimes things aren't worth the battle or getting worked up over, "Pick your battles!" These are the exact words that flipped everything in a different direction for me and my ex. I was and still am very grateful that Corey was able to put that balance in my life and show me a more calming reality to help me move past what isn't important. I now say this out loud to myself before I even think about saying something I don't want to say or don't mean in the heat of the moment. Sometimes, Corey will even give me that "remember what I told you" look, and then I am set right back to square one.

Think strong—be strong! (Joyce Meyer)

My actions changed a lot and not in a bad way. I was determined to not only be a better mother to my son but a better person to myself. I had to reject the sadness, and I had beyond evil things that tried to attack my mind. My family and friends had to see it and hear it from my body; it was not healthy. I said, "I can't settle for this life of pain I'm feeling!" I prayed hard through it and surrendered all my fears to God.

I knew that no weapon formed against me shall prosper because greater is he who is in me than he who is in the world. I am bold, courageous, and confident in Christ. I can do all things through Christ who is my *strength*! God was in the middle of my battles; God showed up in my storm, in the middle of my trouble. He picked me up in the middle of my hopelessness, in my dysfunction. He opened my eyes in faithfulness, with grace and love, and I am forever blessed to know I am never alone, ever! *He* showed up in my storm. He is my captain and constant. He will never fail, and he will never fail in your darkest hour either.

I am a better co-parent and thankfully easier to talk to because my ex and I put Jaxx first, and we have both moved on to a better life for both of us and in healthy relationships that Jaxx can now see two good, happy homes everywhere he goes. That is really all I wanted all along, for him to see happiness and real love behind every door so he could grow up and know what that means, even through the negative parts.

God put my ex-husband in my life for a positive reason. I know he hurt me, and God is the only one who can work on him, not me. Not only did God give me my son, but my ex gave me my son also, and for that I can never forget, and I will have mercy and hope God continues to work on him for Jaxx's sake.

I hope I can inspire you with this vulnerable chapter because we are all made of cracks, and in those cracks, you will always find the light, so embrace the cracks and learn to be vulnerable. God made us with scars, cracks, bruises, and some bumps so we can get something better on the other side of it. A reminder that we made it, and we are better for it.

When Jaxx is older and he asks the questions he needs to ask, I will be honest, and I will be proud to help him through whatever he needs to get him past the confusion, fear, doubt, and whatever else he may be feeling. I never want him to hurt, but it's inevitable that we all do, so we can learn to move past the mud God needs us to walk on. There is no storm impossible to get through, and there is no mountain too high to climb.

This storm is not one that is new and few in this world. I know there are many others out there, men and women who have gone or are currently going through the same valley as I did. Remember to keep pushing through it, and the other side will be brighter for you. It might not make sense now, but it will once you get to that finish line and realize what was on the other side is healthier.

There is always a happy ending just like the Disney movies we all love so much. Mine just involves a cute little boy! What a breath of fresh air it is to have my little man dancing around my new table that God has placed in my new season. This table is better; this table is pure *bliss, and God is at the foot of it!*

Revelation: *Make the decision to cast away the manipulation clouding your mind, whether it's an object or a person. Take a sticky note and write on it, "I will not let manipulation ruin my life." Say it to yourself over and over when it keeps attacking you. Surrender it all and find freedom in letting it go.*

Make Your Mark

Fierce one!

—Missy Rodgers

Everyone has a "trademark." Whether it's a certain mark on your body or a phrase you use daily that everyone knows, that's your thing, and it reminds them of you.

When we are born, we are marked, and we became marked before we opened our eyes into this world. God knew when you needed to be born, so he marked you before your parents even knew you were coming soon. He knew the place you would have in this world and the amazing impact you would put on others, starting with your parents!

My trademark was always singing. I would sing everything as a little girl up until now! Now I just sing my heart out in my home in front of Jaxx and most certainly when I'm alone and nobody is watching my crazy dance moves on top of my couch and bed while using my dry shampoo as my microphone. I chuckled at that one because I literally do this!

For a while in my late twenties, I had my side shaved, and that was a trademark I rocked for a while with designs and constant fresh shaves by my one and only amazing barber and brother. That changed once I had Jaxx and wanted to grow it out, so I chopped all my hair and started fresh! Now I can say Converse is my forever mark. When I worked in the medical field, that was all I wore, every color on a different day. Everyone would ask me, "Don't your feet hurt wearing those all day?" and I would chuckle, saying, "Nope, I will continue to wear them until I'm gray and old!" Now in my business casual job at Hynes, I slide those babies on from time to time to remind myself and those shoes, "I'm still here!"

Not a lot of people know this, unless they know me extremely well, but I have seven different laughs for different reasons. The only person who knows every single one of them and the reasons for each is my brother. You can say that's a huge trademark if you know me and the weird laughs that can come out of my mouth. Once I start laughing about something, I have a hard time stopping! Now when you hear me laugh, you might be hesitant to figure them all out. Good luck!

Know your good trademarks that God put on you when he marked you into this world. Use it for good and don't question yourself too much if you are getting it right like I would do all the time.

God knew my biggest purpose was to be a mother; he knew I needed to have my son to keep pushing, keep pressing on.

My mom has told me time and time again that I had him too early on after I got married, but I beg to differ on that. You see, God put Jaxx in my life and made a huge mark on Jaxx's life and mine when he was born. I will never forget the moment he and I met eye to eye for the first time. Nobody in my mind or around me was in that room except for him and I, and that was the best mark God put in my life and his. You see how God works, he knows every timing in your life and when you need it. The bond is unbreakable. God knew a huge storm was coming my way and to get me through it with strength and a purposeful mindset. Becoming a mother was the only way to help me push forward, even knowing it wasn't going to be a walk in the park. He knew I was able to withstand the pressure I was about to face and that I would stand to tell my story to not only lots of people but also my son, so he could walk in faith with me to become the man of God I know he will be, stand strong, firm, and wise in this crazy world we live in today.

To this day, I still tell my mom and anyone who talks about my story that Jaxx was the best thing God has given me. I am forever blessed, and without God, I wouldn't have him. He made it all possible for me to be his mother.

Don't get me wrong, the single mom life was rough before I met Corey! I wouldn't change it for the world, though. I couldn't ever live with regrets. If I regret anything, then my life would be very different, and my blessings might not be as big as they are now. If I chose to go down a different path, I knew wasn't good for me.

The late nights with Jaxx when he was sick or when he couldn't sleep because he was scared and just wanted to be held by his mama are some of the best moments and bonding times I would cherish with him. I would be dead tired, but I would make sure he was safe and comforted before I would even try to get the sleep I needed for work the next day! I would let the laundry that I needed to fold just lie there and wait because I needed him to be comforted first. Everything in my life was set aside, and to this day, it still is when he needs me.

Being a mother is the best blessing God ever gave me. I am forever grateful that God placed this precious mark on my life.

The Lord will fight for you; you need only to be still. (Exodus 14:14 NIV)

I Am

I am who I am.

—Exodus 3:14

Who are you? Who are you becoming? Who are you trying to please? Who are you praying for? Can you answer these questions with confidence? With purpose? With strength? With grace? It's okay if you can't right now, but you will!

God's I AM is strong and purposeful. There is no fear in his I AM. God's got it so when I think about who I am, I feel better and focused knowing he will deliver; I can handle it in my I AM because of the following:

- *I am a warrior, a giant in my voice.*
- *I am the song that raises my spirit high.*
- *I am going to rise and climb.*
- *I am always ready for my next battle because I am unstoppable.*
- *I am not a failure.*
- *I am going to prosper over and over.*
- *I am going to keep it moving.*
- *I am not average.*
- *I am a part of the focus.*
- *I am the mark he put on my life when he marked me during my hopelessness and worry.*
- *I am a winner.*
- *I am closer to bigger victories.*
- *I am faithful.*
- *I am a woman of God.*

- *I am being transformed.*
- *I am a better mother.*
- *I am a better daughter.*
- *I am a better sister.*
- *I am a better friend.*

What is your I am? Who are you? Post it on sticky note and place it on your mirror to remind yourself just how important you are to not the world but to yourself. Your self-worth is the most important factor you can place on your heart.

God is my door

God said to me, "They have to go through me first before entering your door." He knows the plans and future for me. He knows how to bring the good and take out the bad. He knows when to close my doors and open the next. In order for anyone to enter my life, they must go through him first to go through my next journey, storm, guidance, crossroad, chapter, lessons.

He has brought to me, and for you also, some people you didn't want in your life and put a hole in your heart, including some pain. But he had a purpose for the bad seeds in your path—he knew it was just a little step to get to the next and that the new seed would blossom, to get to the better stone you were and are about to step upon on your mountain climb.

I thank my enemies; I thank God for placing the toxic seeds in my life to get me to the good life I have now. Without them, I wouldn't be able to wake up with a bigger smile, a louder laugh, a better stride, a glorious vision of my future. Thank your enemies because God placed them in your circle to give you a better life. Be more cautious in your lane and stay humble.

The Lord will fight for you; you need only to be still. (Exodus 14:14 NIV)

Go after the stronghold in your life. I am here to keep it moving; keep shining the light on many others that need to see it also.

If God hasn't marked you yet, he will, and I hope he can use me as a vessel to get to you. I feel it in my bones, heart, and my soul that great and amazing things are in your view. I know you see those crossroads and they look scary, but the doors that lie ahead are glorious, so do not be afraid to take your steps. You are not alone during your walk; I will help you take those first few steps you need to take, but just know he will be your guiding light to the rest.

Control your thoughts and be mighty to God because he is mighty to save you. You are a warrior in his eyes, and you are a warrior in mine.

Revelation: *I want you to take a sticky note and write on it, "I am a warrior! I am enough, and I am worthy every morning I get to see a new day."*

If our God is for us, then who can ever stop us, and if our God is with us, then who can stand against us?

Celebrate the Unseen

We all have layers, embrace them!

"How" is the starting place of your spiritual growth; it is how we keep on a constant path of what is coming next into our lives.

One of my biggest problems is that I don't know how to forgive those who have hurt me, and it takes a minute for me to understand why God needs me to forgive. I don't know how to forgive them and keep an appropriate distance from that person without a mental violent block. Yes, I said it, violence in my head! I'm human and sometimes my mind goes into fight-or-flight mode.

The devil will always try to distract or discourage you, knowing he can't defeat you because when you resist him, he will always flee. So when I have those negative thoughts, I say, "Jesus," over again in my mind. Knowing the "I don't know how it is okay right now" is completely normal to not know how certain things will play out. As long as you keep the faith alive in your heart and flee the devil, then you are doing something right, which God knew you had the potential to get to.

At the end of the day, we all have layers, tons of layers, that have been shedding since birth. I know it sounds gross, but it's true! We fall, we feel weak, and then we get right back up for the next battle cry in our path, our trail, our climb, our journey, our tale.

We need to celebrate our success in all the layers of our life. Some layers have been hard to handle, I know! But did it make you stronger? Did you learn a lesson from it? Did it bring you blessings you never thought you would see coming? Did God give you more *yeses* and *amens* in your layers? I know he did it for me, and he's not even close to done with them, and he isn't done with yours either.

God is enough when he can control my life, and he is the only one allowed to control my path and journey. He gave me my boots to climb my mountain. He gave me the strength and willpower to get to the top of each mountain he has given me along with you. If I slip going up my mountain, his hand is right there to help lift me up to the next rock climb because he knows I will stumble going up because that is life, my friends, and that is how we learn to conquer each stride. Do me a favor and do not let anyone control you. Let God control your life. Let him take the wheel. Let him take the next layer off to the new one.

Stay humble in the wisdom of God. He will fill what is empty in your life, and you don't need to know how; you just need to know who, and he is the who in your life. No need to question perfection.

He is my constant and my home in every place I step foot in. When I say that, I mean literally everywhere I go every day! I know when I feel alone, I am not alone at all, and he's near and dear, holding my hand in all my journeys, good and bad.

If you look beneath every surface, every layer has something deeper underneath it. If you don't know what it is, that is okay; you are not supposed to know because you are not the one taking you there. He is taking you there, so enjoy the ride.

Let the redeemed of the Lord tell their story.
(Psalm 107:2)

God is trying to change us in so many ways. We need to let him do what he needs to do in our lives, in our souls, and in our hearts because he knows what's best for us.

I know some of you are stubborn. I know this because I know I am one of the most stubborn of them all. I like to say I'm strong-willed but not really. I have always had a hard time with others telling me certain things, and this is how it is! I'm a perfectionist in my own lane. Now I live with my eyes wide open after everything that has happened in my life, but the only one I let lead me is God. I still try to listen to what my parents say and my close family and friends, but really, when I feel discouraged, I just pray through it knowing God will change the course for me in the right direction I need to fall upon. Sounds scary? Yes, but it's the only way to a brighter future.

I am always going to be a work in progress because every progress that God bestows upon my life is to a brighter future and light into the victory on top! I have more to gain than lose in every battle that hits me in the face. God is my shield from the impact that tries to defeat me. I cannot be defeated when I have someone so mighty in front of me, untouchable!

> *You are my defender, my place of safety in times of trouble.* (Psalm 59:16)

Have you ever thought, *Could this get any worse?* I know I have a lot more times than I could count honestly. If you have said this out loud or even in your head, I want you to know that it absolutely could be worse, but guess what, I know that when I think this, I think that there are so many others who have battles heavier than mine. I am not saying that your battles are not validated, but I want you to stay humble in the good things in your life, that they could be way worse, and if it's bad, just put your mind in your happy place, a moment that made you happy that makes your heart soar every time you think about it. I know my happy place is my son. I went back to holding him in my arms for the first time when everyone in the room in my mind was gone, and it was just him and I, staring at each other, his eyes on mine and mine on his, locking that moment in my heart forever. That moment was the happiest moment of my life and always will be. So when I am in my dark place at home, I will go into his room and think about it, and then my anxiety starts to calm down, and my depression goes from black to white.

If God called you to it, his grace will bring you through it. In every avenue that you take, he will be your sanity. Even in your darkest fears and your darkest waters.

My mind feels like it's on fire when it's cluttered with thoughts that cloud my way. I have to fight that off when it happens, and you need to do the same. I promise you are not crazy when this happens, it's just the enemy is trying to get in your mind and take over, but you can, and you will fight it off.

We can't see what is going to happen next. That is why we need to celebrate every unseen moment, give thanks every morning when we open our eyes to a new day, and give thanks when we close them at night for giving us a glorious day to live through. Even if it was a tough one to battle, it was a day that the Lord let us survive so that the next day will be better, and we can give thanks and praise.

We are not promised tomorrow. That's a huge statement in my life, especially when my dad was getting his open heart, not knowing what was going to happen; God was preparing me to let go. I was scared to death of losing him, and it mentally drained me for weeks even after it was all said and done.

We have no idea if one of our loved ones is going to enter the gates of heaven, so please do me a favor after reading not only this chapter but this book as a whole that you tell all your loved ones you love them before you go to bed tonight, even if you send a simple text or want to get crafty and make them something special and mail it to them, so they have something exciting to open when they get it. Make their day, make them smile, and show them you care, you love them, and that you are always here for them, even during their darkest moments and yours. A little goes a long way for a lot of people, so be that person for them.

> *Praise be to the Lord my rock, who trains my hands for war, my fingers for battle.* (Psalm 144:1)

> *For God speaks again and again, though people do not recognize it. He speaks in dreams, in visions of the night, when deep sleep falls on people as they lie in their beds.* (Job 33:14–15)

Revelation: *Go through that storm, put the life vest on, and hold on tight because God is your captain. You are going to get wet on the ride. That's okay because the sun on the other side will warm you right up when he takes you there. Put on your colorful sticky note, "I will let God stay the captain in my storm, and I will celebrate the unseen!"*

Depression Won't Win

Face everything and run; or face everything and rise!

—Devonne Lindsey, *National Suicide Prevention Lifeline: 1-800-273-8255*

The spirit helps us in our weakness.

—Romans 8:26

Keep taking every day one step at a time, one step closer. Just follow the light out of the darkness. The darkness won't stay, it can't stay. Follow the goodness that is ahead of you, follow the freedom and mercy that is upon your hands while you walk your difficult storm. The waves may be high, but God will calm that wave and carry you. He will mend the broken pieces and wipe every tear from your eyes!

—Anonymous

I will give you rest—everything will be fine for you.

—Exodus 33:14

I am going to throw out some powerful verses in this chapter because depression is a very real, powerful, and a deadly hold the enemy likes to bestow on our hearts. And I'm here to tell you, he won't win this one, he won't! When he grabs at you and belittles your soul to think you aren't good enough to climb and stand tall on your mountain to victory is when you let him win. Please, don't let him win.

I have struggled with depression on so many levels, and it has really dug a deep hole in my life time and time again. I will admit it still can grab ahold of me, but in the name of Jesus, I can't let the devil turn my tables like that because at my table, I have danced the dance many times with the devil sitting in my chair, and I refuse to let him stay when my focus is straight ahead, at the highest peak of my mountaintop that God has laid out for me to climb and reach as high as I want to until all my prayers land in heaven. You can do this also; I have faith in you.

When the heart doesn't feel like it wants to pump any harder, it is when you need to *push* further in the existence of what is right in front of you, and what's right in front of you is the light away from the darkness and away from your enemies who spit on you. Who wants someone to spit on you daily? I know I don't, so I keep pushing, and that's the only way you are going to roll on to freedom. *Keep it moving.* Don't stop now.

Faith always pulls me back in when something dark comes into my light, always! I can't say it enough how much everything that tries to ruin me can't! Even when I think it's done for, I pray through the moment, cry a little because, let's be honest, I'm a very emotional person. I dig deep in my heart and ask myself, *Is this really what you want your life to be like? To feel this way? Are you going to let people make you feel less than what you think you are?* No! I am better than all that, and depression can't and won't ever win. And same goes for you in whatever storm of depression you are sailing in, you can push through it and get to your calming waves.

Sometimes we expect other people to lift us up from every struggle we face, but sometimes we must get up ourselves and know that God is on our side, and we truly are not alone during it. We just need to trust in him and not be afraid to let him carry us. Our parents, siblings, grandparents, cousins, aunts, uncles, they all love us very much and want to help in any way they can, but sometimes they just *can't* do what God can do, and they can't do what *you* can do because I know you are strong enough to get up on your own, talk yourself through it, write it down on a sticky note or journal, go for a run and blare your music in your headphones, or whatever it may be that helps you release that fear inside you that you need to get out! At the end of the day, we can only rely on ourselves and God; that's the hard truth for every single person walking this earth right now! You have to make the change to be the change!

I know a lot of people who work out and run to relieve some stress in their lives, to take their minds off things. Even if it's a body image goal or just the feeling of working out makes them feel good, I always recommend it. If you haven't even tried to go for a walk in your neighborhood, it's a must! I am not big on running, but I love to go on walks in the park or in my neighborhood, either by myself or with my son. I will listen to my music and take it all in, think about what I want to accomplish for the day, or if it's the end of the day, I'll think about the things I need to do better, and then I would also praise myself for the good deeds I did. Along with prayer, amp yourself up a little because you deserve to know the feel-good things you did for the day. It's an amazing meditating thing to do, and music helps even more when doing so. I rate it ten over ten, five stars, my friends. Get those headphones, make a playlist, and go for a run/jog/walk. It'll really help your mind to expand and feel better, along with Handel's Ice Cream afterward.

There is not one person I know who doesn't or hasn't dealt with depression. The scary thing about depression is that something always triggers it. Depression is the trunk of a tree, and the branches are the growth that the trunk is supplied like anxiety, fear, nerves, abandonment, bullying, sexual abuse, suicidal thoughts, unworthiness, drug abuse. All these feelings lead to depression and can spiral you into what I call the unknown or the darkest part of your storm.

You are not alone, and you are not fighting your depression alone either! I can also tell you, you are not in control either. There are nights when I would cry and ask God, "Why me?" I never got an answer or even a thought. He would cross into my mind right at that right moment when I needed it. It made me so frustrated for years and years because depression kept creeping back into my life at the moments I wanted to finally be happy.

God is definitely the captain on my boat in my storms. I am not good at navigating the tough waves because he has complete control over them and my life, so he finally answered my question with a thought in my head one day at work on a random Wednesday afternoon, and that is I need to learn to control my depression and everything that makes it stronger. With that, he means "I will handle all your storms, but when you feel yourself drowning in the moment of fear is when you should not be afraid and surrender it all to me, so I can take it away. And in the meantime, you need to control the wave you are on while I break away the fear for you." I immediately thought of these two short and simple verses in my head:

No fear. (Joshua 1:9)
Quiet! Be still. (Mark 4:39)

These verses help me when I feel anxious or depressed when I am alone, and I hope they can help you during yours. I say them out loud in my head or literally out loud when it gets rough!

Another time during my divorce when I was at my lowest, I just kept thinking all kinds of negative things about myself, like why can't I be or feel loved completely and faithfully? I began to think I wasn't ever going to be good enough and that I wasn't worthy! I prayed to God to please take the negative thoughts away because I knew he was not happy with the fact that I was thinking this way when he loves me so much and I am never alone.

During this time, I was shopping at Target. When I got to my car, I had a double-sided black-and-white card on my windshield. It was not an advertisement or anything like that, just two quotes with positive words, and I looked at all the other cars around me to see if they had the same thing and nobody did but mine. They read:

How beautiful is it to be alive! (Henry Septimus Sutton)

Now and then it's good to pause in our pursuit of happiness and just be happy. (Guillaume Apollinaire)

I keep the card in my car right in front of me as I drive to remind me that God sent this message to me to remind me that I am not alone, and it is good to be alive. Keep fighting and keep climbing.

You may not be able to physically hear God in an audible way, at least I can't, but he is always there to give you a message when you need it most, a sign, and most importantly for me, my visions and thoughts. He lies on my life to help me stay on the clearing path he has laid out for me. I know he is doing it for you also, and he wants you to keep pushing forward during your storm because he has something so much bigger for you on the other side of that huge wave you are trying to get past! Let him be your captain!

I will give you a new heart and put a new spirit
in you, I will remove from you your heart of stone
and give you a better heart of flesh. (Ezekiel 36:26)

People can change for the better or the worse, but you have to let the change embrace your journey. You either learn from it or you don't. Either way, God is going to run your course and swerve it in a different direction for you if you decide to be stubborn, and he will win—he will make it better for you because he wants good for you, not bad! Even if you don't understand why it's happening that way, in his mind it's going perfectly for all the *yeses* and *amens* he is putting in your path, stay patient!

There is always a better solution, and everyone has a different balance in their life to find it. You just take the steps to get to that point. I know it is hard some days, but I have faith in all of you to get to that point in your life where you can step away from whatever is dragging you down. Maybe medication is what helps you, and that's great if you can eventually get off it and survive life without it and find hope in a better tomorrow. But please, don't rely on it to make you a better person. You are already a better person by being in this world that Jesus died for you to be on and for him to get to know you better.

Depression is a serious situation to have on your shoulders. Some do not take it seriously enough that everything that happens in our lives always ends up causing us to have some kind of depressive episode. It may be for a day or two; it may be for years. And if you can't control it, then you are down a bad rabbit hole.

Let's call it temporary depression, even postpartum depression, because I know I still deal with postpartum and my son is already five years old. It's only temporary if we can find the willpower to get up and say, "No! Not today! I am stronger than you!"

There are some days I wake up, and the first thing that hits me when my eyes open is depression. I start crying, and I feel weak to get out of bed. This is usually when I don't have my son and all I want to do is hold him. The first thing I do when I get in this mood is grab either my Bible and open whatever page is in my face and start reading it, or I will put my music on with my AirPods and walk around the house, trying to calm myself down before I even try to start my day in that situation.

I'm lonely, but I'm not alone. (Steven Furtick)

I had a vision when I listened to Pastor Steven Furtick talk about that quote above. I was walking down a very muddy path that I was struggling to get through. God gave me some nice boots to walk through the mud safely, and when my knees buckled, he carried me the whole way. I trust in his truth, and I trust what is behind my next door through that muddy path.

What is it about the boots and mud that he loves so much because, apparently, he likes using this to give me affirmation in my life, almost like I need to really enjoy the mud, rain, and boots—it's a big one for him and I. It is how he likes to connect with me.

Banish anxiety from your heart. (Ecclesiastes 11:10 NIV)

Have you ever been manipulated by anyone in your life? I bet you have, and it sucked a lot. It made you feel a little crazy in your mind. Let me explain what a manipulator is in my mind and how

I can break it down, what they do to your mind, what it did to my mind.

Manipulate as defined online says, "*Fragments of a broken bone into the correct position.*" Let me break this down for you…a manipulator will take your bones, break them with their manipulating words, and position them the way they want your body and mind to think and feel. I felt this on so many levels. When I looked this up, it really hit home for me on how manipulated I was during my marriage and especially during the divorce. Once I got a grasp on it, I took charge and didn't let the manipulation control my life anymore. I put a shield on my heart when anyone who tried to manipulate me came into play, and I mean everyone including family.

If you are being manipulated and it has put a big dark hole in your life, you need to try with all your heart and soul to let go of it and say, "No! You will not and cannot control my mind anymore!"

My family and friends would tell me how manipulation was controlling my life, how bad it was for the longest time. It really was the worst part of my battle, storm, and depression. It made me think I was the worst person, a hopeless soul, and brought a lot of fear into my daily life. I needed to get the strength to push it away and fight back. I fought back during my prayers, and with the faith of God, I told myself I will not tolerate this anymore, and I will not tolerate the pain because I am better than the enemy!

This dark part of your life will not stay; it will not be permanent! It's going to get better and better, and when it gets good, there will be so many *yeses* and *amens* in your light, along with even more blessings you didn't see coming to your table. You are going to make it because that good part is tremendously awakening. Every good thing has a dark part, so go through the dark when he wants you to get there, so you can see the light in the crack and watch it expand to something wider. Don't give up, have grace, praise and mercy on the ones that hurt you. I know it's hard, but the hard parts will mend to a stronger, healing process for you to walk again, get out of bed stronger, talk better, think wiser! You are important, you are loved!

Revelation: "*We must go through many hardships to enter the kingdom of God*" (Acts 14:22).

You are enough. Repeat that over and over! "I am enough." Put that on a sticky note and stick it on your mirror, stick it on your fridge, stick it on your planner you write in every day. Keep it going.

May 2021

I was lost but now I'm found.

May 2021 changed my life and one I will never forget. I am not proud of this moment, but it is one that still gives me chills.

It was a Wednesday, and my divorce was coming up in a few months to get finalized along with Jaxx's birthday ending and the first one I didn't get to be with him all day and celebrate. He was only two years old, and all I wanted was to hold Jaxx every night, and this night I needed him. I cried all day at work. I knew I should have left, but my coworker was keeping my mind busy, and the last thing I needed was to go home.

I was on some heavy antidepressants, and I was not using them the right way. I was supposed to take one as needed and with no alcohol. I was at the point of taking two, sometimes four, a day and drinking alcohol with them when I was alone. I would never ever do it when I had my son, but on the weekends and during the week when it was me, myself, and I, it was a constant battle to take my pills and have a drink. I wanted to numb my mind and stop crying, but it just wasn't working. I was going to church a lot on Wednesday nights after work, and this Wednesday, I was not having it. I wanted to go home and have a bottle of wine with the thought of finishing off those leftover pills, which was more than four.

I got home, and something gravitated me to get dressed and go to church. Even though I didn't want to, but a little thought said, *Go!* and I did. Let me just say, nobody knew me at this church, I was new, and nobody there knew my personal life and what I was going through, let alone that I was on antidepressants. It was close to the end of the service, and we sang worship for a while. Then the pastor stopped and asked, "Does somebody have a court hearing coming up?" He was in such deep thought and looked bothered. Nobody was saying anything, and I knew I had one in two months coming up. He kept repeating the question, determined to find out who it was. I raised my hand, and he ushered me to come forward. I was so nervous I could have puked right then and there; my eyes were swollen from crying all day and feeling broken, shattered! I went up there, and he just kept looking bothered and sad.

He said, "Honey, the Holy Spirit is telling me you take prescription medicine."

I replied in shock, "Yes, I take antidepressants."

He said, "Are you abusing them? The Holy Spirit is telling me you are, and you need to stop before it's too late."

There was not one single person who knew this, and I stood there shaking, crying, praying because I knew, I knew there was a reason I was there that night, and it saved my life! That is a fact!

The pastor's wife came up to me after he prayed on me, and she said, "I just see carpenter bees all around you. Your whole life they just keep coming after you, but you just keep swatting at them. I need you to keep swatting and don't stop."

The emotions in my soul were indescribable. That was a once-in-a-lifetime experience and not just a sign but the Holy Spirit directly saving my life and giving me a wake-up call.

I went home, and the first thing I did when I walked into my apartment before even putting my purse down or shoes off was go to that bottle and dump the remainder that I wanted to take that night down the drain. Not a lick of alcohol hit my lips that night either. I prayed, I wrote, and I thanked God for being so good to me time and time again, even when I feel like I have completely failed him, even when the things I was thinking and doing were probably making him so angry. But he never gave up on me; he knew the purpose was to get up and keep going. I was and am bigger than the fear I was feeling that Wednesday in May of 2021, and after that, I completely changed my outlook. Even though I was working on becoming better within myself and finding that self-love I needed in my life, that moment rocked my world to the core, and I never looked back.

I never have thoughts of wanting to get on any kind of pill to help me cope anymore. I will never do that even if I think I have a clear conscience. I have figured out too many ways to help me get out of ever feeling that way, and it's not a good road to go on. It's scary!

All I kept thinking after that was Jaxx needed me, and I needed to make him proud. I needed to show him he could grow up strong, wise, and can conquer anything he put his mind to. I was not feeling like a good role model, so thank you, Lord, for being the forever-and-always savior in my life. I don't want Jaxx to grow up thinking that's the outlet to feeling better. That is not the end result, and that is not what God is calling him to do or for anyone else who has gone down the same road I did.

This situation is bigger than me, but God is bigger than any situation you face, so don't face it with fear because this is your battle cry that God will carry you through—he carried me through mine. He will carry you through the mountains, the fire, the valleys, the storm, the waves, the traffic, the thunder, the climb, the cancer, the disease, the mental illness, the depression, the negative thoughts because he is bigger than all of that. You don't have to like the journey he is putting you on; you just need to be okay to understand it. I did not like the journey in May of 2021 because it was one that could have taken me away from everything, and God knew this was not the purpose of my life. He was bigger than those pills and alcohol, and he still is.

He put me through everything so that I could have it all. My level of happiness and faith is all in his hands, and I am forever grateful for all the burns I had to endure to have the power to heal them because he gave me the strength to get up and walk.

During this tremendous battle, I was not distracted by his love for me. I was distracted by the pain I was feeling, and if I was ever going to get out of it while praying, it would get better. He handles all of it, and I have learned to become completely distracted with his work in my life. I thought I could become the editor of my life for years, and I was not the editor in my decisions because the respect I had on myself was not worthy to stay, so he let me know he is the author in everyone's life. We are lethal to our own thoughts, so editing our chapters is not the calling he has stored in our lives. Learn to let go and be okay with what he and she said, how you got treated, how you lost that job, and I promise you when you learn to let go, the author of your life will turn every page into the miracle you prayed for if you learn to say, "I'm done," and let him work. He holds the pen.

These are my authentic, real, and rare chapters, and I'm blessed to be able to share them with all of you. The chapters in this book had to go through him first because he is my true editor in all these pages and with me, all my life through what is to come next in my journey. *I see that mountain, and I am not scared to climb it, and this is a tall one and one that took a lot of courage for me to start climbing. But I am blessed you are here with to walk through the pages that I trusted him to let me write.*

Remember, you always have the support even when they all leave, and when the rest stay, God will always stay and see you through it. It may hurt a lot in the moments that feel like your world is shook up, but that storm will pass, and you will see that valley to victory. Don't lose faith in what keeps you going and hold onto it tight.

I thought I was losing faith before I went to that church, and I was pulled into the most amazing faith I have ever experienced in my entire life, glorified in the light and away from the darkness. It changed every bone in my body, and I didn't ache as much when I dumped those pills down the drain. It was liberating and freeing to say that God saved my life that night; he used every power to get to me, and it worked. The pastor was determined to find out who it was that he needed to call up to that usher. There was no getting out of that one, and I am thankful for that moment and one I will never forget.

You are the new seed planted in the soil and his growing plant of abundance, love, and joy! Everyone is a perennial plant that grows back every spring—we always bloom, and we always will. He will keep watering your life, so you grow taller every year!

Revelation: *What was your saving grace moment in your life? Write it down on your sticky note, and remember, what happened to you is in the rearview mirror now, you don't live it anymore.*

Transformation

Don't look behind you—climb.

Do you have a sibling that you would do absolutely anything for, younger or older? It doesn't matter because you are connected and always will be. It's a bond and love like no other.

My brother means the world to me, and since I knew I was going to be a sister, I knew it was going to be quite an adventure ahead, and it was.

He was born June 12, 1994, and he was the cutest baby that looked like a precious moment for the longest time. He was full of energy, and he brought to every room lots of excitement when he walked in. He could turn a story into a comedic stand-up show and have us all laughing into tears. This is no joke, the funniest one in the family for sure.

But with that laughter and smile came a story behind the eyes he was hiding for years since birth, a challenge he was facing that we as a family knew nothing about and something we will truly not know how he did, and does, feel to this day if you aren't currently experiencing it yourself. All we could do was show support and learn what and how we could do that. With the amount of love I have for him, that was easy!

To my dear brother

Dear Brother,

This chapter is dedicated to you, for you, and only you—so you can read and keep forever the words I so dearly keep close to my heart every day of my life. I want you to treasure this chapter and be reminded how amazing you are even on the days that are rough. Maybe something to reference back to and know that I got you and remind yourself you are going to be okay.

We have had a lot of interesting road trips, valleys, and doors together, and I wouldn't change any of them. Yes, even the sad parts and angry ones. That is what builds character and what molds us to who we both are today.

I am so proud of you, Brother—you are one strong soul, and I admire you for the steps, climb, swim, run that you have made in your life and still do to this day. I look up to a good number of people in my life for their strides but yours takes the cake to a whole different level.

You are an amazing father to your three boys, and you love your wife endlessly. You are a good man, and your heart is pure. Even if words and sadness have ever gotten in the way of anything, I know the love for family is strong in your heart and always will be. Don't ever let go of that.

Siblings will be siblings, and through the many laughs have come a lot of setbacks for us, only in times we felt very strongly about our situations, and that's okay. We are all allowed to feel things deeply and some have been misunderstandings, miscommunication, stubbornness, sadness, depression, and lots of anxiety.

Do you remember when I was having that massive panic attack working at Biotest when I was pregnant with Jaxx? You knew exactly what to do for me, and that was to grab me tight and let me cry, along with trying to calm me down when I was a mess. You understood so much how I was feeling even without words, and all it took was that bond to make me stop and put myself back together—you left and grabbed me some ice cream and all was well. I know Jaxx was very happy! But all in all, just that moment I will never forget and only the love of two siblings can understand what works and what doesn't.

I am convinced we were twins in another life. The way we grew up and our thoughts came naturally—we could look at each other and know exactly what we both were thinking at the same time. I'd call you and ask, "Are you okay? I have a feeling something is wrong," and you'd immediately tell me what was going on like I already knew right then and there. I still know to this day when something is off, but we are all grown now, living busy lives, but just always remember I am a phone call away and there is nothing I am doing that will be too busy to be there for you. We have to stick together through thick and thin, even when we are not happy with each other; we are inseparable and always will be.

Growing up, I didn't care that you liked to be rough and tough with toys. I was just happy to have a sibling to play with—I did not care about the G.I. Joe dolls and Hot Wheels (now all I play with is Hot Wheels with Jaxx) because I admired having someone next to me, growing up with, and being there through all the challenges and achievements we conquered with each other. That is really all that matters in the end, that we grow up healthy, happy, and learn from the storms we tread through.

I admire you beyond words, and it makes me very emotional to even fathom sadness or pain you've endured growing up and sometimes currently. I don't know if it is me being an older, protective sister, but just know the older you got, the more I knew you'd be okay with having your own little family; it has brought you so much peace even when distance with us had to happen. Knowing you're happy and free is what sets my soul at ease.

Don't ever think for a second you are not loved because if you ever feel that way, know you are loved by me, and there is nothing in this world that can take that away from me, or for you! When you are scared, I will shield you. When you can't breathe, I will breathe for you. When you can't see, I will search for you. When you are hurt, I will mend your pieces. There is nothing you need to do alone as long as you have me.

Brother, I love you; I support your every journey and avenue God puts you on because he knew you were strong enough for all the valleys and doors he put in front of you. I know the purpose of your mountain is very high, but you have the strength of a million men, and you are stronger than the unthinkable to climb your mountain to the top. If I meet you up there first, I promise I will extend my hands to you always and help with that last step to your victory battle cry. I hope you choose to dance and always stay golden!

I love you endlessly,
Sister

Final words

He has been blessed with so much perseverance and support from his family that I know some families don't do for their loved ones, and some children don't go home to the love and support that they so desperately need. My brother serves as a beacon of hope and empowerment for others who love him, and his contagious smile and laugh is always engraved in our hearts. He may have been through a lot of muddy waters in his wake, but he is bigger than all the storms he has been through—he is more than the fear, tears, anger, confusion, frustration, doubt, depression, anxiety, illness, and everything else that came along with the storm he walked through so effortlessly!

My family and I witnessed a brilliant human being who walks this earth not only masking pain he endured for years since he was four but that he still masks to this day. His self-discovery and courage to be his authentic self is powerful, and I look up to him for it, and you should also! Anyone and everyone who truly knows the kind of person my brother is knows everything I have said so far is accurate to a tee. Even on the days when he is not himself, I know in my heart who he is, and I love him for all that every day for the rest of his life.

Revelation: *Do you have a sibling who struggles with a tough battle? Have you witnessed heartache with them? If so, write on a sticky note a prayer that will help guide them to peace and always remember to show and continue to hold their hand through any pain they are going through—they need you the most just like you need them!*

Self-Discovery

The best view comes after the hardest climb.

Steven Furtick's new book, *Do the New You,* was a game changer for me with six of his awesome mindsets that I want to reflect on how they changed the way I think and how it can hopefully help in your life as well. Let this be a domino effect to paying it forward to positivity and reflection on your self-discovery.

I'm not stuck unless I stop

I had a lot of moments in my journeys when I felt stuck and lost, not knowing what turn to make next, stuck in that crossroads. I didn't want to stay stuck, so I prayed through to God that he would help me in my times of need, to get me unstuck. And when there's a will, there's always a way! A way right through that crossroad to a continuing path to my next chapter—this chapter!

Steven's chapter really led me to reflect on all my stuck moments, that I am never really stuck when I have all I need right in front of me and that he gets me unstuck in the mud, which he has proven time and time again on helping me out of. I hope you are led to get unstuck. Just keep that faith in your heart and don't stop. Free yourself so he can help you through your challenging stuck moments.

Christ is in me. I am enough

This one helped me in so many different ways and is one of the strongest areas of the mindset.

My whole life, faith has preserved the greatest but listening closely to Christ gave me all the freedom to know. Regardless of all my seasons, in all of them, I am always enough because Christ is in me defending every outcome I face, good and bad. There is nothing in this world that can win at making me think I am not enough. He knows better than to let that kind of mindset control me, and he is doing the same for you *every day!* Even when you don't think it is happening, it is every minute of every day!

Faith is stronger than a hundred mountains around you because every climb brings you closer to all the faith you have inside you. Just allow it to happen and you will be set free.

With God there is always a way, and by faith I will find it

Why do we sleep where we hide? When in hiding we lose sight of finding our way to the light that's right in front of us.

Before I met Corey, I was lost in a dark pit, and if you know him, then you know he has about a million flashlights in our home, so the best way I can describe how he found me was with all those flashlights. He said, "Come on, let's find the way out together," and off we went.

I was hibernating for a while, and with God, he brought Corey to me so I could find the light I needed. He knew and knows to this day I have enough faith to find any light that comes toward me in any darkness I face.

When you find yourself hiding away and pushing everything away, use your faith to find the way. If you feel weak to stand, he will pick you up and carry you out. Just extend your heart to him, and he will make a way.

Your faith is always bigger than your fear and your purpose is stronger.

God is not against me, but he's in it with me, working through me, fighting for me

Have you ever had a day, week, month, or a year of thinking everyone is against you? I know I have and sometimes I still do, but with this mindset Steven wrote about let me know even if everyone is against me—*let them* because God is never against my battles and seasons. He's always with me, working through me and most of all fighting for me. I could be stranded in the desert with no weapons while all my enemies come trying to attack me, but they can't because God is my weapon and my shield. If my bronze bow is lost in the fire, God becomes my bow and fights for me harder than anything I will ever encounter.

What weapon do you use to help you fight your battles? Whatever your answer is, if it isn't God, your weapon won't be strong enough. You don't need armor when he's in front of you, defending you.

When that battle is done, he will lead you to the next door, so trust that doorknob you are about to grab for your new season.

My joy is my job

When I think of joy, I think of the joy on Jaxx's face when he gets excited about the little things. I think, *Is it that simple?* It sure is because, as a five-year-old, we all looked at joy in the same simplicity, not even realizing it.

I see the smile and joy in his eyes, and I'm immediately filled with all of it myself because I brought that little bundle of joy into this world—God let that joy in my life and the opportunity for it to be my job to guide him. That's my joy, and it's the greatest and my biggest blessing that I won't take for granted.

What is your joy? Does it bring you peace? And does it feel like a blessing? If so, that's your permanent joy, and it's your job to never let that go. That is the gift that keeps on giving, and God made sure to bestow that joy in your heart.

If you feel like you haven't reached it yet or know what your joy is, I promise you it's there. Let me hold your hand and help you find it. I'll be your flashlight when you feel lost to find your joy. Let's turn that pain into power!

God has given me everything I need for the season I'm in

After reading Steven's last chapter and mindset, it became the strongest one to end such a powerful book of knowledge. The words say it all, *"God has given me everything."* I love that to pieces because he has and still does when the pain was hard to endure. Leaving me sleepless, he still gave me everything I'll need and more. He gave me all the love and signs to push me through the seasons and valleys.

When you don't understand your own strength, know the strength comes from him and nothing else, and when you don't have the words, stay silent and let him speak for you. He gives you everything you need in all the preparations for the light ahead.

Who am I? The new Jenni, who is the woman of God mighty to keep fighting strong with him by my side. I was once weak, but now I am found and stronger than ever. *Thank you, Steven Furtick, for this life-changing book for myself, and I hope it inspires others to feel brand-new!*

Revelation: *Take note and put on your sticky note: "Unstuck, Enough, Faith, Fighter, Joy, and Everything." You are all these things, and you deserve to shine!*

Potholes

Don't let that hole stop you from continuing to keep moving.

I live in Ohio, and the potholes are always bad where I am from. Everyone that knows prepares for them after winter is done, when the salt eats away what used to be a normal road, which is now looking like we are going straight down to Chinatown!

We swerve and we panic when we can't get past them, hoping and praying this isn't going to be an endgame on my tire and/or rim because I am already running behind, and this is the last thing I need right now to start or end my day. Car problems can make for a bad day.

I learned something about these potholes that put my life into some perspective on how we can look at them.

You see, there are potholes we don't see coming, right? Some are so big you are just praying your tire is okay, along with ones that look big but really aren't, so you took that chance to drive through it knowing you could have swerved with no other cars around you. It is all on the angle and how you are focused on what is ahead of you. You never know how deep they are, and others really are completely unavoidable and inevitable to even try and get past, so with faith, you just drive through.

Life is just like all these potholes that unexpectedly approach our lives. Some are huge and some small, but we eventually get past it and move on. We fix what may be broken, and it might cost us a lot of money to renew, but in the end we see we are still intact and God got us through that. Even if we left us a little stressed or nervous, you pulled through and began a new day.

What inspired me to start this chapter was when Corey was traveling to Stuart, Florida, on his bike to help his brother move out there. He was hours ahead of them and closer to their stop to Georgia, but hours before getting there and close to the sun setting, he noticed he had someone behind him who was driving a little too close for his liking, and he was looking in his mirrors to keep an eye on them before at the last minute noticing a massive pothole that was approaching. With only seconds to think, it was either swerve and not know if the person behind him would be paying attention to him or go right through the hole and chance getting his tire destroyed, maybe even worse an accident. He chanced the hole with seconds to spare and *bam!* That rim was bent and tire flat, leaving him on the side of the road trying to bang his rim back in place, air in his tire, and getting back on the road to get to Georgia.

Okay, yes, anyone reading this is probably thinking, *Is he crazy? Why wouldn't he wait for his brother or call someone to trailer it?* Safety first, right? Well, this is Corey, and anyone who knows him knows trailering is not an option, so he monitored that tire, stopped when he had to for more air, and hit his rim until he got to Georgia! *Relief* for us all tracking his location.

The next morning, he got up before everyone else to get a head start to finish to Florida, going sixty to sixty-five miles per hour until he could get it to a shop. He tried to find someone to get a new tire and rim before he would have to get back on the road in three days to head back home! We all thought, *Okay, if he can't get a tire and rim, there is no way he is going that far coming home, especially with possible storms on the way.* But nope, he was riding it regardless.

With a lot of prayers on my end, he was able to get that tire and rim on the day before he had to leave, and safety was on his side the whole way home.

The reason I wanted to tell this story was because Corey did not let that pothole discourage him from continuing to keep on moving, even when everyone was telling him to stop and do the right thing to stay safe! He knew he was going to be fine, putting faith out there that if something didn't feel safe, he knew his limit to stop and do the right thing. He never let the pothole win; his road ahead was still good, and he never let defeat get the best of him. God guided him, and he was shielded the whole time. He knew Corey was going to hit that pothole. He knew swerving was not going to be an option because maybe swerving was going to cause a horrific accident that would leave him not kneeling there with a hammer to fix his rim. I am grateful for the pothole that may have saved his life at that moment.

I am not saying you need to hit all the potholes and that's the source to all your problems. I wanted to use this as a metaphor to how life is for all of us, that the battles you hit are like potholes, but you can still get out of that hole you are in and keep going just like Corey did and what brought him home to me and his family! He was still intact, and he still got that new tire and rim. We prayed he would get to come home okay.

Make the right judgements in your life and know that you aren't alone when choosing what may be the right swerve or going straight ahead into the unknown. In reality, God guides the purpose on what happens next so go into that reality that it's going to be all right, and if it's not in that moment, then have faith that the end result will turn out to make sense and be okay.

Corey was not happy to have a bent rim and air coming out of his tire with every bump he hit, but he didn't let that discourage him from getting to where he needed to be. God made sure of that!

Are you afraid of those potholes? Do you always swerve past them, or are you putting faith that God will get you through them? Whether it is a personal struggle or a family crisis, always remember there is no pothole in your life that God can't get you out of. Even if that tire goes flat, God will make a way to mend it and prepare a new one for you.

When we are on the bike, I don't see what is ahead of us; I put all my faith in Corey because I know he isn't alone in guiding us to safety. Others may be nervous knowing we are on the bike and praying we get to our destination in one piece, but I hope they read this knowing we are always in good hands.

We are not promised tomorrow, but we have to have a glimpse of hope that when we get a new day, we don't take it for granted.

Revelation: *My pothole is getting through my anxiety when I feel overwhelmed. While it is hard to move past that hole, God helps me move through it. What is your pothole challenge, and how is God moving you on that bump ahead? Write it on a sticky note and remind yourself you are better than that pothole and all the other ones ahead of you!*

Comma

He will wipe every tear from their eyes.

—Revelations 21:4

Life is like a comma; it just keeps going to the next one until that sentence needs to end. I look at life that way and every battle we come across; every curveball thrown our way is a comma.

Comma: *A punctuation mark (,) indicating a pause between parts of a sentence. It is also used to separate items in a list and to mark the place of thousands in a large numeral.*

We should pause during our commas in life to reflect what is happening around us, as in processing the moments that are affecting our thoughts and how we react to them in a negative or positive way!

When my comma hits me in my sentences in life and journey, I pray through it. It's how I cope and how I get through the battle at that time. Some of my commas are severe, and I don't know how to handle them; and some are minor, and it's just a tiny wave in my wake. Regardless, praying on it every day is how I breathe better and what calms my anxiety before it gets too large.

Some days, we want our commas to end and the period or exclamation point to approach, but that's not how life works, and that's not how our stories play out, family and friends. We must embrace this comma and learn to love it in the moment, even when it gets sticky and, to be frank, scary at times.

You may be in the middle of a rough storm, but just remember that comma won't be there forever before God is going to pull you from the waves. He is not afraid of your situation in your storm. Even if you are afraid, he wants you to not be afraid. Trust in him and stay calm in the middle of it.

I have had a lot of storms, and I felt like I was drowning every single time. Many times, I didn't want to keep going. I didn't think I was strong enough. I felt weak and afraid of everything. God didn't like the way I was thinking, and he made sure to put my mind in a different gear shift because that's not the path he had planned for me, so he kept my comma in play, kept me strong through it with the power of prayer to get me up every morning to a new day to another conquering victory.

Every single victory I climbed made me a stronger woman of God and, to this day, a better mom, daughter, sister, and friend. I thank God for my commas and my storms because without them, I wouldn't be the person I am today. Trust me, it took years to look at myself with confidence, a lot of tears, a lot of anger, a lot of negativity and frustration. I hated who I was seeing in the mirror, who I thought I was becoming because I felt unworthy and questioned why so many awful things kept happening to me. I was becoming something better. I was becoming a glowing inspiration not only for myself but for my son, my family, and anyone who needed a positive outlook in life, to shed some light on the dark parts—and nobody likes the dark parts. But the darkness always has a light at the end of it, and I promise you, you will find yours. God will make sure that light is there; he doesn't want to see you suffer. He loves you so much and wants to see your light blossom into something beautiful! We should stay calm and be still during the storm, embrace your comma, and love the journey it's putting you in. The end result is always better than the beginning.

When God walks in the room, demons flee! The light comes, and he heals all the pain you are feeling. Even for that moment, he will heal your heart and carry you.

Do not let your heart be troubled and do not be afraid. (John 14:27)

I love this verse so much! When I feel troubled, anxious, or in pain, my heart seriously feels like it's ripping. They talk about how your heart can literally break and you can feel it—it's so true. I have felt my heart tear, but this verse calms my heart and lets me know I don't have to be afraid because God would never let me live with a troubled heart and a broken one at that; he picks up the pieces and mends it back together time and time again.

Stand firm and you will win life. (Luke 21:19)

Another one that reaches into my soul and picks me up; *standing firm* makes me feel strong and *winning at life* makes me want to live again even when I didn't feel like living is worth it! Don't let the enemy win because you are stronger than the enemy that tries to burn your bridge.

I knew the only one who is going to protect me and has since before I was born is my God. I don't need to worry or think too hard about what is going to happen next or if it am going to be good or bad because I surrender all my fear to him, knowing and trusting that he would make everything okay for not only myself but for Jaxx. He is my constant over and over!

Keep people in your life that are in your corner, and I mean positive people who love and support all your dreams and goals, will listen, and not judge, care for you even on your worst days. I have gained and lost people in my life I loved—some broke my heart, some I walked away from knowing it was what needed to happen for me to grow. All in all, it was all for the purpose of growing into the flower you need to be and what God called you to do because, once again, he will never fail you. Even on the days and nights when you think he isn't on your side, he is and always will be on your side, rooting for you the loudest!

He is so good, and he knows how to calm the waters when my brain is like crashing waves. He knows when I'm going to have a panic attack before it happens, and he already knows what he is going to do to take it away.

> *The heartfelt counsel of a friend is as sweet as*
> *perfume and incense.* (Proverbs 27:9)

When I am at my weak points and the devil whispers in my ear, "You're not strong enough to withstand the storm," I will pray, "In the name of Jesus, GO AWAY!" I refuse to have that negative mindset in my head. I know that when I let it stay, I am put in a very dark hole, and sometimes it takes a while to crawl out to the light. So it's very important I stay on a steady path of positivity and keep the devil out of my head pace when he tries to enter. He will only try to enter when he sees weakness, but sorry not sorry, devil, I am stronger than you. You are also stronger than any bad seed that tries to make you weak. This is how you need to push forward in your times of struggle and in your comma moments. God isn't finished with your life and your journey; he is just getting started, and all the *yes* moments he has given you already is just the beginning to more *yes* moments you are about to experience, along with being ten times better than you ever imagined. When he gives you a *no*, do not be discouraged because that *no* is bringing you to an amazing *yes* and *amen*!

> *The size of your storm tells me something about*
> *your importance.* (Pastor Steven Furtick)

I've had people tell me their storm was a couple days to seven years, and I'm here to tell you that no matter how long your storm lasts, how big the waves get, God will never let you drown. At the end of your storm will come the most amazing victory, and you will look at yourself and breathe better than you ever could imagine.

The storms come with many doors that cross our paths and seasons. I'm telling you *tons* of doors. I can't even count how many doors opened and slammed in my face. I am blessed for a lot of my doors that closed in front of me. I didn't understand it at the time and got frustrated why certain ones had to go, but as time passed, my storms calmed down, and my commas became periods to end that chapter in my life. I was fearful to see other doors open. I was afraid it was something that was going to hurt me. Guess what? A lot of them did hurt me, and it stung really bad, but I got back up and let them sting me over and over, and I kept swatting at those carpenter bees my whole life until I could reach the end of that door to my next one that God had planned for me—to get to the better destination, my rally cry, my victory, the brighter light to the next brighter light that was and still is coming. He's not done with me yet!

I had nights when crying was all I could do. I would cry until my eyes would swell and make myself physically ill. Why did I want to do that to myself? I asked God so many times, "Why would you let this happen to me?" I was so angry and bitter. Even though I've been through this same hoop, door, and storm before, I was still just as upset. I would look and think of myself in a negative way. I had moments of feeling completely paralyzed. God would speak to me in so many ways to make me stronger. He carried me when I couldn't walk, and he got me up every morning to my beautiful baby boy every day when I had him. You see, that's what gave me my strength. It wasn't just the strength of God but what God gave me to keep me strong! When he started my chapter and comma at the beginning of Jaxx's life, he knew there could be no end to the journey with my son, even when I leave this earth one day. That's the beauty of the comma journey, my friends… Embrace that comma God has given you because each one has something beautiful in each story and each storm that passes! It's ugly at first, but it always comes back stronger and more beautiful.

> *Casting all your anxieties on him, because he cares for you.* (1 Peter 5:7)

When I have an anxiety attack and I think we have all experienced this more than once in our lives, it can be intense. I know mine put me in shock, and I needed to walk away, release it, and come back to reality. When you have anxiety on a daily, surrender it all to God, and he will take it away. It might not be right away, but just keep breathing and keep praying through it, so he can take you out of that storm. He will take the ink and end that comma to a new sentence. He holds the key to your life, so trust in him and do not be afraid. Release that anxiety and surrender it.

> *Fix your thoughts on what is true and honorable, and right, and pure, and lovely, and admirable.* (Philippians 4:8)

Remember when I said the song "Oceans (Where Feet May Fail)" is my anthem song? Well, here are the lyrics below that take me to where I need to be. I hope this helps you to find peace as well:

> *You call me out upon the waters,*
> *the great unknown where feet may fail.*
> *And there I find you in the mystery,*
> *in oceans deep, my faith will stand!*
> *And I will call upon your name,*
> *and keep my eyes above the waves,*
> *when oceans rise, my soul will rest in your embrace,*
> *I am yours; and you are mine!*
> *Spirit lead me where my trust is without waters,*
> *let me walk upon the waters wherever you would call me,*
> *take me deeper than my feet could ever wander*
> *and my faith will be made stronger in the presence of my savior!*

God took my healing song and made it into a purposeful vision for me to the path he has made real. I am so blessed and humbled for the life he is leading me on.

> *The Lord will fight for you, and you must be quiet.* (Exodus 14:14)

Who knows if perhaps you were made queen
for just such a time as this. (Esther 4:14)

*"If you were born with the weakness to fall, then you were born
with the strength to rise."* This quote came to me years ago from someone unknown, and I live by it, and I want you to live by it because we
all fall, we all have scars and stories to tell that have made us stronger, but most importantly those scars are what gave us the strength
to *rise*! We were born with weakness, so we could learn to get up
stronger and not be weak, to prosper through the fire and come out
untouched. *Rise up unafraid!*

You are a warrior. You may have a shelfful of books in your life
with thousands of chapters, and if you go back and read those chapters in your past, you are reliving some pain! Trust me, going back
to the pain I've been through in my life has taken me to some dark
thoughts, but I said, "I am stronger than the negative thoughts in my
mind. That chapter is closed!" Your chapter is closed also. Embrace
those books that are on your shelf with all those commas. Look at
your books and say, "I am better now because of you. You gave me
grace!" Nobody is perfect, but we will get better after every battle.
We are warriors, my friends. If you think you aren't strong enough,
remember God is your strength—he will lift you up high!

My scars are proof of his power. (Pastor Steven
Furtick)

We all bleed, but it's not how you bleed! *What* do you bleed? Do
you bleed love, grace, anger, bitterness, depression, anxiety, fearful-
ness, sadness, guilt, worry, happiness, worship? I can tell you I've bled
all of that. I have bled and shed a lot; I've recalibrated my mind to get
in a better mindset in the circle of my life. You see, we have this thing
called *our minds*; it's so powerful, and it can really take us down to a
bad place and bring us to what we bleed. Our heart pumps the blood
in our veins and what keeps us alive, so tell me, what do you bleed?
Is it always something negative? Do you blame your life on a family
member? Is your road taking you on a bumpy road that has a bunch

of potholes you can't swerve? Let me tell you right now, your road is not going to be perfect, but the road ahead, I promise, is going to be an amazing crossroad that is going to be more than what you thought you could accomplish in becoming the person you are meant to be. You will bleed goodness, mercy, and grace!

How do you take the right path? Think about it…when you deal with a difficult person in front of you, are you going to stay frustrated and stay out of control? Or are you going to smile and say, "It's okay, I understand your difficult battle because I've been there!" We are too quick to judge and hold a grudge when we need to understand we are all climbing a mountain to the top. We are all on our boat during a storm, whether it's big or small! I am guilty of holding grudges and getting upset, wondering why this person hurt me like that. Why did I deserve that? But I've also prayed more for the ones who have hurt me, more than myself, and that takes a lot of strength! You know why? Because they were a part of my *commas* in life, in my chapters, in my books, in my path, in my storm, in my mountain, in my climb, in my stepping stones, in my boundaries—everywhere I have ever stepped on, I have prayed for my enemies in my commas! It hurt, it was difficult, but afterward I felt better. I felt relieved. I felt lighter. I felt like I could walk, talk, sing, sleep better when I learned to embrace that comma my enemies entered my valley! If I can do it, you can do the same thing for your enemies.

> *The spirit helps us in our weakness, we do not know what we ought to pray for but the spirit himself intercedes for us.* (Romans 8:26)

> *Don't be afraid; just believe.* (Mark 5:36)

I want you all to *rise*. I want you all to see your *victory*, embrace every single crossroad life is giving you. Even when it's hard, please free yourself and let him do his work. Let go of the pain, let go of whoever put pain on your heart and who crushed your soul because I promise you that pain is going to give you a better future when you least expect it. Don't hold onto that darkness in your room. Reach for that light in the crack. *Reach* and sing out your battle cry! God is working on the ones that hurt you; they need grace just as much, and it's not our will to help them. God just needs them to stay away from us so we can heal, and he can do what he can to give them beauty in their ashes.

Embrace your comma, say hi to it, smile at it because the good part of that comma is so much bigger. The chance for greatness is a page and chapter away. Be patient because you are going to get *good* in your mind quick when that comma takes a spin into your greater future. Keep your eyes up and don't lose sight of what is up there for you.

I know what's good for you; you are not alone in the darkness of that storm in your battle. I have and still will face many more of them and so will you. For now embrace the wave because what's behind it, the most beautiful sunset to a brighter future. Love that *comma, you battle cry warriors!*

Revelations: *Write on a sticky note your most powerful comma, your hardest comma, your best comma, and your most challenging comma. Then write what each one taught you and how it made you stronger. How did you prosper from it?*

Bloom

Be like a flower and blossom.

Children of the future,

I hope you grow up wise, grow up strong, and grow up wild. Your hearts now are innocent, and as you get older, you will see different shades of colors. The ones you see now are vibrant with a crisp of gold, and once you get wiser, they fade just a little bit as the leaves of your tree get taller. As long as you keep your hope and faith alive, they truly stay bright, and those branches grow long, high, and untouchable.

With any heartbreak that walks your path, I need you to hold onto that child at heart and know that we all saw everything in a different way when we just learned how to walk; we all savored those imaginary thoughts, thinking one day it would all come true. Nothing felt out of reach when you were a child, and I pray you stay this way and not let any heartbreak define who you are inside, who God created you to be.

When you sit with your grandparents, take it all in, learn from every memory they share. They are the hope that can keep all generations alive. They are the ones who help mold your innocent mind to life. Do not take any of it for granted. And love your parents with all your heart. Let them hold you and never let go for one day they will be gone, and we will miss that tender hug and the loving whispers of "I love you." Let them continue to lead you while God continues to work on you.

If you have a sibling or siblings, let them be your best friend, for there is no better friend than the one who shares it all with you and knows everything you go through, from beginning to end! I love my brother with all my heart, and even when we feel far away from each other, we are never far away, even with unspoken words. Whether you are a sister or brother, the oldest or youngest, hold onto all those sibling memories and build off it and learn from each other. You never know how much you need them when the going gets tough.

Don't hold anything back and run with it, run until you can't see what is behind you. Whether you sacrificed it all to get through that door and maybe need to leave some things behind to see the other side, go with confidence knowing it is the only way that you will find happiness. God will see you through it; he will make sure you are being carried. Please do not be afraid of the storms that will come along with it. It will only make you stronger. God will and would never give you anything he knows you can't handle. If you have to cry, let it out but let it go and give it all to him, so he can move you, mold you, and begin to finish the blossoming journey he has started upon you.

If there is anything I wish I did when I was younger and that I hope for you is you allow daily affirmations in your life, every morning or every night—fill your mind with positivity first thing in the morning or first thing before you shut your eyes. I wish I did this when I was a little girl and started at a young age to help me start my day because it has done wonders in my life now. Regardless that bridge we all must walk on was going to happen, I just wish I would have had a little bit more preparation to be nicer to my mind, so I didn't hurt it so much while crossing it.

He will make a way to pull you out of any shadow and into the light. Just have faith in him and don't ever let go of that.

Stay creative and do whatever your creative mind likes to do—don't lose sight of it. And I don't mean just painting and drawing, I am talking about anything that frees your creative mind into that happy place you love to go to. This can be singing, dancing, poetry, crafts of all kinds, sports, organization from planners, book organizing, gardening, and planting, the list can go on and on. Once God leads you and sets you into that creative mind, then it is all up from there.

You are going to go through your first heartbreak and definitely more than one. If I can give you any advice on this, please go with an open heart that God will continue to lead every broken heart you will encounter, so you can get to the right one. You have to learn what heartbreak feels like in order to know what it feels like to never have it again. Your soulmate will go through the same obstacles, and when you are together, you will both understand this journey because God led you both to each other in the timing he has made it known. He knows years and years beyond what is coming into your life; he just asks that you don't get too discouraged and put all your faith into what he has in store for you.

Travel, and I mean see everything you can. If that means taking that school trip to going someplace new every year and seeing all the things you can take with you, then go. I do a lot of traveling now and see things I can because we aren't promised tomorrow, and I want to say I saw all the views I wanted to see. There is nothing more humbling than what God has created around us, what he made beautiful, and we should all take the time to cherish it. Take advantage of that vacation time or that family getaway with pictures, laughs, and take it all in. You won't regret any of it when you look back say, "I did that!"

Stay confident in who you are, and I don't mean just on the outside but be true to yourself on the inside. Be kind to your heart; it's beating for a reason! Nobody can take your calling because God called you to it and nobody else; not your parents, your grandparents, your siblings, aunts, uncles, teachers—just God. If he calls you to it, take it because he is better than anything. He is the superior of all things good. He is your comfort zone, the calm in your crisis. And when you are angry and feel like screaming, do it but don't forget to breathe through it. God knows every thought you are thinking, and he is there to help slow it down in the midst of the screams and the fear; he is there to take that all away.

A chain is only as strong as its weakest link, and you, my child, are not the weakest link, and that chain will be free. The Lord is here to develop you and not the enemy to destroy you! It's not a dead end; it's an open road, and I pray you trust every windy road. When you stop in that boat, I hope you trust your sails. When you want to run, don't compare it to someone else's run and stay focused on your circle. Sit where you are supposed to sit, climb the mountain you're supposed to climb, and rest your head where it is supposed to lie. Don't hover over your frustration because when you believe in something and can't let go of it, then you become something great!

I reached out and asked some family and friends to give me one inspirational word that has helped them in their lives, and these are the words I received: *faith, determination, confidence, gratitude, communication, survive, grace, and honesty.*

How powerful is that I read just those one-word answers and thought how strong they all mean; not only to my life but knowing that each word has a story behind it for that individual, that they went through something to give them that one word to help them through their darkest moments, their sailboat in the storm. They may have all lost an oar, but during it, they used God's grace and love to get through it.

My one inspirational word that gets me through is faith, and it is tattooed on my wrist so it's a reminder that faith is what gets me through every day I get to wake up. With faith I am stronger than I have ever been, and with faith I can do anything I put my mind to. There is nothing stronger than keeping it close to my heart and knowing one word can help every single destiny God bestows into my storm. Because I am not afraid of the storms anymore, and I want you to not be afraid either as you grow up and learn to fly, as your small wings turn into towers! *Don't be afraid* of those waves; they are only waves and nothing more. You are greater than the roar! Let *peace* be still in your wake.

Go in faith and love. Speak your mind and say what you feel in all aspects of your life. Rise up and feel well in knowing the calling you have inside you was born with you since the beginning, that when you cried your first battle cry when you were born, that it was and always will be the strongest one you will ever encounter because it was God's will for you to be here. And it is his calling that you do great things.

I love you. I love you even when you are still going to be afraid. It is how we learn. Trust me, every step you take and every milestone you walk is going to be scary; that is life and that is how we keep going. I need people like you in my life because we need each other. We are all a community together, so keep encouraging one another.

I am always here for you all. I know God's calling for me was to be an advocate of words to get to you all, to hopefully give you words of wisdom to help you stand taller, breathe better, walk lighter, fear less, smile wider, laugh louder, and climb that mountain. Because remember, it's always going to be the mountain you need to climb. Don't be discouraged on how high it is, just *keep going*! I have all the *faith* in the world for all your little *beautiful souls*!

Love you to the moon and back,
Jenni

Revelation: *Write on a sticky note your one word of inspiration that helps you in all your darkest hours. What word do you say to get you up and going? What word stops the crying, stops the heartache! Confirm that word and make it your loudest battle cry!*

Acknowledgments

Dear readers,

As I reflect on the journey of writing Battle Cry, *I am filled with profound gratitude for the countless individuals whose support and encouragement have made this endeavor possible.*

First and foremost, I extend my heartfelt appreciation to my family and friends for their unwavering love, patience, and understanding throughout the writing process. Their belief in me and their willingness to listen to my stories have been a source of inspiration and strength.

I am deeply thankful to the love of my life, Corey, who offered invaluable guidance, feedback, and encouragement along the way. Your love, insights, and perspectives have enriched the pages of this memoir and helped shape it into its final form.

I am grateful to Jaxx for inspiring me to be a better mom every day of my life and being the motivation I need time and time again to climb the mountain I needed to conquer every page in this book.

Finally, to the readers of Battle Cry, *thank you for embarking on this journey with me. It is my sincere hope that the stories contained within these pages resonate with you, inspire you, and perhaps even offer a glimpse into the shared humanity that connects us all.*

With deepest appreciation,
Jenni

About the Author

Jenni is passionate about helping others with her memoir, *Battle Cry*, along with her mission to empower individuals to discover and embrace their true potential, self-discovery, and growth.

After facing many storms since childhood, Jenni embarked on a profound journey of transformation, which is vividly captured in her memoir, *Battle Cry*. Through candid storytelling and heartfelt insights, Jenni shares the highs and lows of her path to personal empowerment, offering readers a relatable and inspiring narrative.

When not writing, Jenni enjoys sightseeing on the Harley with her boyfriend, Corey; spending time with her son, Jaxx; being with family and friends; reading; traveling; and continuously seeking new ways to grow and inspire others. She lives in Canfield, Ohio, with Corey and Jaxx.

Battle Cry is Jenni's first memoir, a testament to her dedication to helping others transform their lives and realize their fullest potential, climbing their highest mountain, persevering their storms, and opening the doors to their greatest prosperous journeys ahead.

Printed in the USA
CPSIA information can be obtained
at www.ICGtesting.com
CBHW060747201124
17649CB00044B/1026